More great, original do-it-yourself projects
in the same series:

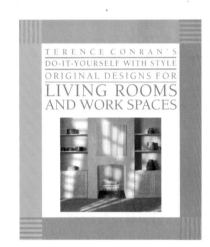

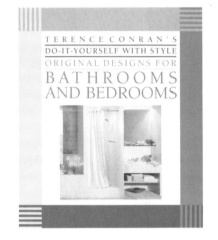

PROJECTS
Alcove Shelves and Cupboards
Radiator Cover
Wall of Display Shelving
Workbench
Tool Cupboard
Home Office
Workroom Ideas
Replacing Baseboards
Glass Shelves

PROJECTS
Tiled Bathroom: Bathtub Unit
Shower Unit
Basin Unit
Paneled Bathroom
Towel Rod
Wardrobe with Hinged Doors
Folding Screen
Japanese Wardrobe
Bed with Trundle Drawer

TERENCE CONRAN'S
DO-IT-YOURSELF WITH STYLE
ORIGINAL DESIGNS FOR
KITCHENS AND DINING ROOMS

CONSULTING EDITORS
JOHN McGOWAN AND ROGER DuBERN
PROJECT PHOTOGRAPHY BY HUGH JOHNSON

A FIRESIDE BOOK
PUBLISHED BY SIMON & SCHUSTER INC.
NEW YORK LONDON TORONTO SYDNEY TOKYO

F

FIRESIDE
Simon & Schuster Building
Rockefeller Center
1230 Avenue of the Americas
New York, New York 10020

First published in 1989 in Great Britain by
Conran Octopus Limited
37 Shelton Street, London WC2H 9HN

10 9 8 7 6 5 4 3 2 1

Library of Congress Cataloging in Publication Data

Conran, Terence.
    [Do-it-yourself with style]
    Terence Conran's do-it-yourself with style : original designs for
kitchens and dining rooms / photography by Hugh Johnson.
        p.   cm.
    "A Fireside book."
    Includes index.
    ISBN 0-671-68718-2
    1. Kitchens.   2. Dining rooms.   3. Interior decoration.
I. Johnson, Hugh.   II. Title.   III. Title: Do-it-yourself with
style.
NK2117.K5C64   1989
643'.3--dc20   89-11610
                                              CIP

The publisher would like to thank the following companies
for supplying material for photography:

32 Franke Ltd, The Conran Shop, David Mellor Design Ltd,
Divertimenti, Philips Major Appliances Ltd, The Kitchen
Range, Neff Ltd, Stephen Long Antiques, W H Newson & Sons
Ltd; **34** Aston-Matthews Ltd, W H Newson & Sons Ltd, David
Mellor Ltd, Heal & Sons Ltd; **37** The Conran Shop, Neff
Ltd; **60** The Conran Shop.

Project Editor JOANNA BRADSHAW
Assistant Editor SIMON WILLIS
Copy Editor RICHARD DAWES
U.S. Consultants RAY PORFILIO, MILES HERTER

Art Editor MERYL LLOYD
Design Assistant ALISON SHACKLETON
Illustrator PAUL BRYANT
Visualizer JEAN MORLEY

Photographer HUGH JOHNSON
Photographic Stylist CLAIRE LLOYD
Photographic Assistants SIMON LEE, PETER WILLETT

Picture Research NADINE BAZAR
Production SHANE LASK, SONYA SIBBONS

PUBLISHER'S ACKNOWLEDGMENTS
The publisher would like to thank the following for their
invaluable assistance in producing this book:

The Conran Studios, Julie Drake, Rebecca Verrill,
Malcolm Harold and all at Benchmark Woodworking
Limited, Tabby Riley and Alex Wilcock.

The projects in this book were specially built by SEAN SUTCLIFFE
of Benchmark Woodworking Limited.

Special thanks to PAUL BRYANT for his superb original illustrations.

PLEASE NOTE
Before embarking on any major building work on your home,
you should check the law concerning building regulations and
planning. It is also important to obtain specialist advice
on plumbing, gas, and electricity, before attempting any
alterations to these services yourself.
    While we have made every effort to ensure that all the
information contained in this book is correct, the publisher
cannot be held responsible for any loss, damage, or injury
caused by reliance on such information.

DIMENSIONS
Do not mix imperial and metric when you are making a calculation.

Typeset by Servis Filmsetting Limited
Printed and bound in Italy by Amilcare Pizzi SpA

CONTENTS

Projects

INTRODUCTION

By designing and building your own kitchen which is very often the most important room in the house, you will get more satisfaction from it than any off-the-shelf kitchen can ever give. The final result will be a kitchen that is tailored exactly to your own requirements in terms of style and practicality.

As you plan your kitchen, you should consider many alternatives until you know precisely what you want to achieve. On the following pages are many inspirational ideas and suggestions for kitchens and utility rooms which can be adapted to your own design. In addition, there is a complete kitchen, and utility room units, to build yourself as well as many original and classic designs for kitchen fittings from plate racks to display shelves. Begin with a minor project if you lack confidence and skill, and gradually build up your hand-made kitchen.

Whether you are creating a whole kitchen from scratch, improving an existing one, or merely adding a wooden knife rack, building it yourself gives your kitchen a truly personal element. It also provides an opportunity to have kitchen fixtures you know are well designed and well built.

Terence Conran.

ASSESSING THE WORKLOAD

The level of change you wish to make to a kitchen will depend upon a number of factors. If you want your kitchen completely replaced and redesigned you must consider just how much you are capable of doing. Building and installing new units, worksurfaces, and shelves is not beyond the skills of most do-it-yourself enthusiasts. However, if you are intending to redesign the layout and move services – water and waste piping, electrical outlets, light fixtures, and gas fixtures – then the undertaking is considerable. In addition, you must consider the legal restrictions imposed upon work involving gas, water, and electricity. It is often illegal and possibly dangerous for you to undertake it yourself.

The moving of units will disrupt existing flooring, tiling, and plasterwork. And while your own capabilities may stretch to woodworking and decorating, they might not enable you to lay floors and replaster walls. Budget for professional help as necessary and get estimates before you start work so that you do not begin with a grand plan and run out of money half way through.

If you are relatively happy with the position and capacity of existing units but are unable to live with the style, then consider revamping them with new doors and worksurfaces.

Small changes can often be made to transform an existing kitchen completely: a new set of shelves for displaying kitchen

ASSESSING AND PLANNING

Building a complete, coordinated, and fully fitted kitchen such as this one in natural wood (above) requires careful planning. Moving fixtures can involve new plumbing and rewiring, both of which will require professional assistance and costly upheaval. The time, effort, cost, and skills required to create such a kitchen must be honestly assessed before work begins to avoid problems later.

There are plenty of smaller projects to undertake in the kitchen. Perhaps the most simple, functional, visually effective, and easily assembled is a stainless steel hanging bar (previous page). Pots, pans, and other cooking utensils hang from butchers' hooks. The bar can be attached between two kitchen units or two walls, or can be suspended from the ceiling.

objects, or a plate rack in natural wood, for example. Another simple device is a steel hanging bar for storing everything from pie slicers to saucepans, making the kitchen a more practical place to cook in.

Once you have decided exactly what you want to undertake, map out a schedule and a budget. You may find that you cannot afford the time or the money to do all the work immediately, in which case decide on priorities. Include in your budget an amount in excess of the cost of materials and professional help as a contingency against possible problems – say ten percent on top of your basic estimate.

Consider well in advance the amount of disruption that will be caused to what is a major room in your home. Will you be able to continue to use the kitchen while it is being redesigned? Other arrangements may have to be made for cooking. Prepare your family for the mess that will result from the work. Above all consider safety, particularly if children are likely to use the area while work is in progress.

You will enjoy the work and be pleased with the results if you have not undertaken more than you can handle. Make sure that you have purchased all the materials necessary for each stage of the process before you start, and that you have the right tools for the job. Finishing, detailing, and decorating can take more time, effort, and expense than actual construction, but are important and must never be underestimated.

FORM AND FUNCTION

As you plan your new kitchen, or make alterations to an existing one, always consider how you want the room to function and to look when finished. The beauty of this kitchen is the quality of the materials used – natural wood, mosaic tiles, and marble – combined with a simple yet elegant design. It is effective because it has been made with faultless precision and a great deal of attention to detail. There are no brackets to break the graphic line of the shelves, no decorative detail to detract from its minimal style, and nothing is placed on show unless it is as attractive as the kitchen itself.

MATERIAL EFFECTS

More than anything else, it is the materials which you choose for your kitchen fixtures that will influence the overall feel and appearance of the room. Let us consider two basic styles of kitchen and the materials which fashion them.

In recent years, kitchens used on an industrial scale – in restaurants, hotels, and other places where cooking is quite literally an industry – have become a powerful influence on domestic kitchens.

An industrial-looking kitchen tends to have a formal, high-tech atmosphere, streamlined and sleek in appearance, with an emphasis on efficiency and hygiene. The two qualities valued most by professional chefs are durability and ease of cleaning. It is not easy to turn the industrial kitchen into part of the living room nor to make it cozy. This is a style for a separate kitchen – a serious cooking cen-

ter, where rustic ideas are inappropriate. This does not mean, however, that an industrial influence will make your kitchen look like the inside of a laboratory or chemical plant. It does mean using high quality materials with a minimum of decorative detailing. Walls are faced with white ceramic tiles, and can extend to the ceiling, have a painted wall area above them, or be broken up for variety's sake with bands of colored tiles.

Stainless steel is indisputably the most popular choice for professional-looking worktops. Very easy to clean and thus hygienic, stainless steel wears gracefully and looks attractive even when it has been scratched and lost its gleam. Stainless steel is quite expensive, however, and can be substituted by laminates or a worktop made from white ceramic tiles, terrazzo (marble chips), or granite.

PROFESSIONAL POLISH

Borrow ideas from professional kitchens when planning which materials to use in a kitchen. In this large and luxurious arrangement, created for some very serious cooking indeed (above right), the style is strictly professional and incorporates an enormous extractor hood, double swing doors, and an open charcoal grill. The materials are functional, durable, and attractive, not homely and decorative.

In a smaller kitchen and on a small domestic scale, similarly strong materials can be equally effective (above left). Stainless steel has been used for professional-looking fixtures, and marble slip tiles provide a hardwearing floor.

Many domestic kitchens these days double as eating rooms and living rooms, and it is common for members of a household to spend a great deal of time there. If you plan to use your kitchen for this purpose, it needs to look and feel livable with a more cozy atmosphere.

Natural materials are marvelous for this type of kitchen: they look and feel welcoming as well as elegant, and the great popularity of the country-style kitchen bears this out. Wood, stone, terrazzo, granite, and slate are generally more tolerant of all the knocks, scratches, and dirt stains which occur naturally in a kitchen than are manmade materials, which scar and deteriorate rather than age gracefully. Even though marble stains if oil or alcohol touches its surface, it retains a pleasing patina of age; but if a white laminate suffers a deep stain, it sits upon the surface as an unsightly scar. Wood that is chipped, scratched, or stained will appear comfortably lived in, while old laminates will start to break up and disintegrate after a lot of wear. Wooden worksurfaces will last longer if a tough hardwood such as beech is used. Obviously, synthetics have their advantages and can be used effectively, and a lot less expensively, in a kitchen or dining room than natural materials. Tiled and vitreous-enameled surfaces are other options which age well and are durable. Most people will use some laminate surfaces in their kitchen and it is worthwhile considering juxtaposing them with, for instance, an old wooden kitchen table, or a weathered butcher's block. Such a contrast of old with new, natural with synthetic, is highly effective and invariably interesting.

SURFACE COORDINATION

The gleaming appeal of polished stainless steel has been enhanced in this kitchen (above left) by choosing only steel utensils and then storing them on a stainless steel hanging bar. The colors in the kitchen are muted and the design is plain so that the room has a studied coordination about it.

Another kitchen (above right) shares this overall approach of coordination but has been achieved using different materials. Simple bricks, painted white, form the basis of the kitchen. The storage units are finished in white laminate, and the floor is warm terracotta quarry tiles. These elements blend well with the wooden high shelf and the large basket above the stove.

MATERIAL EFFECTS

UNDERSTATED ELEGANCE

Gleaming terrazzo (stone and marble chips set in concrete) on the worktop, the palest wood for units, doors, and floor, and muted shades on other surfaces and objects, give this kitchen its understated elegance (right). A small open-plan kitchen shows a truly original design, which could be achieved by doing-it-yourself (below left). Warm, natural, polished wood has been used for the plate rack, worktop, and floor. The doors and units are painted in a pale finish. In a separate, small galley kitchen (below right), the paint on the walls and doors is again pale. It offsets the rich finish of the terrazzo worktop which incorporates a section of wood to act as a built-in chopping board – easily achieved and highly practical.

HAND FINISHED

Doing-it-yourself means implementing original ideas using unusual materials and finishes. One-room living in an open-plan loft (opposite above) dictates that only a corner is available for use as a kitchen. This design could be equally effective in an office, workshop, or studio. Concrete blocks form the base of the island unit which is topped with a laminated worktop. The blocks echo the rough-cast concrete of the walls. All the materials used here are strong and basic like the building they are placed in.

In a small space, such as this attic kitchen (opposite below left), contrasting surfaces could be unattractive, so the wood paneling on the sloping walls has been bleached to match and blend with the wooden worktop.

A useful pass-through from kitchen to dining room (opposite below center) incorporates an attractive closet. The kitchen is beautifully finished in wood paneling which has been painted a clear, bright eau de nil, a color which continues beyond the pass-through to the dining room. The whole door panels stand out in strong geometric relief.

When the kitchen is on show (opposite below right), the appearance is very important. Anyone would be happy to eat and relax next to this line of white units with their marble worktop and a wall of marble slips (tiles).

KITCHEN LAYOUT

Finalizing the exact location of every unit and appliance in your kitchen involves careful planning at an early stage to avoid problems later on. A kitchen is, first of all, a work area, so you should make sure that it will be easy and efficient to use. You should check the location of your doors and lights, then calculate how best to arrange the areas intended for food preparation, cooking, and eating. Bear in mind that you will want to have your cooking utensils within easy reach, saucepans near to the stove, and so on.

If there are children about, make certain that any electrical outlets and open shelves will be safely out of reach. Storage should also be considered before you set to work; think about how much space you will need for cleaning and laundry equipment, cutlery, dishes, laundry products, and food.

As you begin to plan your layout, give thought also to what outside doors can let in – muddy boots and drafts for example – and weigh these disadvantages with the positive reasons for having an outside door in the kitchen: easy access to a garden or a trash can, and to fresh air. How these elements affect your kitchen design depends on how you want to use your kitchen. Some people prefer to be left on their own while working in the kitchen; others love having people wandering in and out, making the kitchen the social center of their home.

If you own a lot of attractive kitchen equipment, think about building a special shelving system to display it to advantage. As with a row of cups hanging on hooks, great esthetic pleasure can be derived from allowing a kitchen's function to determine its form or shape. Do also consider, though, that anything displayed in a kitchen accumulates grease and dust, so think about cleaning chores too as you finalize the plans for your kitchen.

While kitchens should be designed to encourage easy cooking and mobility, the particular plan you choose will depend on your own preferences.

There are five basic floor plans. One is the linear or single-line kitchen, with everything lined up against one wall — excellent if the wall is long enough or if the kitchen is basically a passage. The galley or corridor kitchen, arranged along two facing walls, should have the sink and the stove on the same side of the kitchen and give enough room for bending down – at least 48in (1200mm) between the facing units. Such a kitchen is not recommended unless built against a dead end or a window. The L-shape kitchen is very popular – deservedly, for it combines well with a living or dining area in the kitchen and makes good use of limited wall space. A U-shaped kitchen is ideal for a small area, like an alcove, and offers one of the most convenient and adaptable arrangements of space for preparation and cooking; usually the worktops here run in an unbroken sequence, and one leg of the U can be used to divide the room, with an eating area beyond it. Lastly, there is an island kitchen, a favorite with professional or very confident cooks who appreciate its adaptability and the way it can display their culinary prowess; an island unit can also act as a room divider.

The sink should be positioned at the center of a kitchen, beneath a window if possible (for natural light), not in a corner where it is difficult to get at. It should have food preparation areas on either side. Since moving a sink requires plumbing alterations, you may wish to leave your sink where it is, regardless of placement.

The strong, geometric lines of a modern building have been reflected in this architect's design for the kitchen. Gleaming white units and shelves, in big, chunky shapes house only white, black, chrome, and yellow objects.

KITCHEN LAYOUT

We have mentioned the five commonly used kitchen layouts, but there is no need to stick rigidly to any of these plans. In nearly all kitchens there is a vast potential for flexible space management, using the differing heights of base units, shelving, and built-in or free-standing stoves.

Central islands in particular provide opportunities both to divide a kitchen and to focus attention on the cooking going on there – if so desired. Breakfast bars can serve this function just as effectively as island cooking centers but in a different way – by clearly marking out the cooking from the eating areas. If there is room in your kitchen, it is always best to make some clear distinction between the two.

The sink, stove, and preparation areas, along with the refrigerator, should form a "work triangle" whose sides when combined should not exceed 20–23ft (6–7m) in length. This results in having no two work centers more than a double arm-span apart, to avoid needless exhaustion. Nor should they be uncomfortably close, which would cause cramping. A cramped kitchen can lead to accidents, so plan the layout to allow more than one person at a time to move around the room safely.

Cooktops should *not* be placed under windows – someone could get burned trying to open the window. Neither should a cooktop or a stove come at the end of a run of cabinets – it is best to have a worktop on either side of it, although it could be placed in a corner.

You should also consider the washing machine, if this is going to be in the kitchen. Washing machines do have a tendency to leak or flood at least once in their lifetime, so bear this in mind when planning drainage and choosing a floor covering. For plumbing reasons, if both a washing machine and a dishwasher are planned for your kitchen it is best to keep them close together and near the sink.

AROUND THE KITCHEN TABLE

A niche has been carved in a storage unit for slotting a round table into neat and secure alignment with the open display storage of this small kitchen (opposite above).

Purposefully combining old and new can be very attractive as in this standard, modern, white kitchen (opposite below). The polished wood floor complements a rustic wooden table. It has been placed at an interesting angle for practical reasons as well as for visual interest.

If the table is to be used for more formal occasions, it is best separated from the working kitchen. A screen (above) has been built in as part of the kitchen. The table is a neat extension of that screen, so is linked to, but effectively separated from, the kitchen itself.

CORNER KITCHEN

In a tight narrow corner, precise planning and a design with an eye to detail are required to make the best use of what small space there is (left). Here, there are neatly arranged fixtures and a maximum amount of storage space.

KITCHEN LIGHTING

In kitchens even more than in other rooms, imaginative lighting is essential, so plan it from the start. Natural light sources should be considered first. Think carefully about what will be placed near a window or glazed door and whether it will benefit from sunshine and a view. The sink may or may not require this privilege. A table could be more deserving if you intend to sit there regularly. General electric lighting for kitchens should aim to give the maximum adaptability – and lights should be able to be directed differently for different activities. Avoid a single central ceiling light, because of the shadows it will throw on worksurfaces as well as its marked lack of esthetic appeal.

Worksurfaces must be highlighted for safe and efficient food preparation – fluorescent tubes built into wall-mounted cabinets avoid the problem of the cook working in his or her own shadow. Check that the light bulbs will be hidden from both sitting and standing eye-levels.

Systems of track holding a number of lights with separate switches are useful in kitchens, as are pivoting hinged fixtures mounted under kitchen wall cabinets to provide downward illumination on to worksurfaces. If you also eat often in the kitchen in the evenings, put in a dimmer control to fade out all the kitchen clutter by the sink and worksurfaces when you are eating.

There are many different types of lighting fixtures and bulbs. Fluorescent bulbs use less electricity and last far longer than incandescent bulbs. However, they not only give an unattractive light but have the disadvantage of flickering slightly which many find unpleasant. They also emit an irritating hum.

Incandescent bulbs, also available as track lights, are preferable except where it is vital to avoid the heat they give off or where long life is essential. They range usually from 40 to 150 watts in lighting power. Incandescent lamps can shatter from thermal shock if splashed with cold water and so need completely enclosed fixtures near wet or steamy places, above a sink or cooktop, for example.

Low-voltage tungsten halogen is excellent in kitchens, particularly in the form of small spots. It gives a clear, white light and makes glass, china, ceramics, chrome, and metal truly gleam.

Tungsten strips installed below shelves prevent a large handsome hood casting a shadow over the cooktop (above left).

Knocking out the walls of a kitchen has allowed natural light into an otherwise dark corner (above right), and downlighters have been installed at strategic points.

A small kitchen in a corridor has the benefit of French doors that lead to the garden and provide natural light (opposite). Underneath closets, strip lights illuminate the worksurface and downlighters add extra light elsewhere.

SCREENING AND SEPARATING

Today, modern kitchens are at the heart of family life, and modern cooks do not want to be locked away surrounded by pots while the rest of the family and/or guests are talking elsewhere. Yet some division between cooking and eating areas is desirable. To mark this division without isolating the cook, several approaches have been evolved.

Island units, sometimes containing a stove, are an obvious way of dividing the cooking and eating/living areas, as are units jutting out in peninsular forms. Such plans guard the work triangle from interruption while allowing the cook to take part in any conversation. Often, a peninsular unit can double as a breakfast bar, which makes it easier for food to be served hot from the stove. Most breakfast bars are at worktop height (36in [915mm]), so bar stools are required. Clearly these are not very safe for young children, nor comfortable for the elderly.

The simplest screen is a purpose-built partition made with wood stud and finished to match your kitchen decoration. It can be of any height to suit your kitchen design. You can incorporate storage and display into the structure with a high shelf for display, shelves on one or both sides, or attach hooks or a wire mesh for hanging utensils and pans.

Other forms of screening can be devised, utilizing whatever appeals to you and what you happen to have, such as pots, pans, or bottles of preserved fruits. If, however, you plan on having, and often using, a separate dining room, think about installing a pass-through between the kitchen and dining room. When shut, this will leave the dining room as a quiet room and keep especially pungent smells inside the kitchen. When open, the cook can talk fairly easily to the rest of the household and pass through dishes with the minimum delay.

COUNTER DIVIDERS

In two spacious open-plan areas (above), the kitchen is separated from the main room with a breakfast bar. This has been simply achieved by installing a worktop which overlaps a basic unit on the side facing into the main room, so creating a space beneath it for sitting and for storing stools. By adding a sink to this worktop, plates can be cleared easily from the main room to this counter, which has a dishwashing machine below it on the kitchen side.

COOK'S PASS-THROUGH

In this unusual arrangement (opposite), a pass-through between kitchen and dining room runs directly behind the cooktop. Designed for a virtuoso cook rather than a busy family, it allows direct delivery of sizzling hot dishes to the table. Behind the cooktop, a simple island unit, consisting of a stack of drawers, has an extended wooden worktop which effectively divides the kitchen and provides chopping and preparation space close to the stove.

A Place for Everything

If you like a generally informal, cozy approach to your kitchen style, remember that the general clutter this may well entail requires a large space. If you have only a small kitchen, perhaps of the galley type, you will have to impose a certain discipline to make controlled use of a space in which only one person can cook. In such a case, a more high-tech and practical design may be appropriate.

If you do have a spacious kitchen, you can afford to spread out expansively, but take care that your kitchen does not become chaotic and unattractive. An informal arrangement can create in effect a still-life of fruits, vegetables, pots, dishes, and attractive kitchen utensils.

A Welsh dresser, although the most well-known, is by no means the only way of displaying objects of interest, charm, or beauty. Think about building pigeon-holes to store and display spice or herb jars, interesting old bottles – or interesting new ones for that matter. Despite the potential that space gives you for disorder, try to arrange objects neatly and in a manner that is appealing to the eye. If uncertain about what to display, work on the principle – if you've got it, show it!

Shelf edge-banding (a strip of hardwood fastened to the front edge of the shelf) adds support which can be useful for long shelves. Both shelf edge-banding and back battens are essential if you are intending to store heavy objects, such as casserole dishes. Place on the highest shelves those things you use infrequently. Always incorporate an extra-wide edge-banding that projects slightly above the shelf to prevent objects falling down.

Although it seems obvious, it is difficult to overemphasize the importance of really strong and secure attachments for all wall cabinets and shelves, especially when heavy crockery or pots and pans are going to be stored on them.

AN ORDERLY DISPLAY

Where space for storage is limited, a kitchen has been allowed to extend into a hallway (opposite above). Here an entire wall has been given over to open shelves. Cleverly but very simply designed and constructed, this unit echoes the open shelves in the kitchen beyond, and fills the wall, framing an existing window. The arrangement works well because of the order the shelves impose. They are narrow and placed at varying depths to accommodate certain items precisely, so that clutter cannot accumulate and everything is clearly accessible and easily found. The supports form partitions which ensure that the storage is grouped so that a wide range of objects can be placed together without looking haphazard, cluttered, or randomly arranged.

IN A STRAIGHT LINE

Shelves placed so that they follow the contours of a room, and are regularly spaced, provide a strong geometric grid for neat open displays. A pigeon-hole effect allows for a formal display (opposite below left) of china and glass. Each square is self contained and highlights the objects it houses.

Another simple but highly effective design (opposite below right), with fiberboard and laminated shelves on battens across an alcove, contains a more relaxed display of everyday dishes and glass.

SMART JARS

Dried foods, when stored in large glass storage jars in neat rows, look extremely attractive, and give a kitchen a traditional atmosphere. Storage jars remind us of old-fashioned shops and wholesome home cooking. Here (left) they are displayed to great effect on a custom-made unit which blends perfectly with its surroundings. It is made from simple wood or fiberboard and covered in white tiles so that it appears to be part of the wall it stands on. The depths of the three shelves match precisely the height of the jars. Antique salt containers and old olive oil bottles standing on polished wood add to the traditional effect.

FLOORING

Bear in mind when choosing the particular type of floor covering for your kitchen that it should reflect and enhance the style of the rest of the kitchen – starkly modern white tiles could be out of place in a farmhouse style kitchen, for example. A floor is a crucial influence on a kitchen. The type of flooring you decide on will be partly dictated to you by the sort of subfloor you have underneath. Although there are ways around the problem, you may not be able to put terracotta or ceramic tiles on top of wooden joists, as lumber bends and moves, potentially causing cracking of the tile joints or even of the actual tiles. Equally, if you choose

sheet vinyl or vinyl tiles – both common floor coverings – cold, potentially damp concrete or stone underneath will require particleboard or hardboard as sub-flooring beneath it. You may be restricted by not being on solid foundations or by needing to insulate sound from the level below.

Be careful that the floor of a kitchen in an older building is not too uneven and that it relates properly to the levels of adjoining rooms. Any abrupt change of level could be dangerous as well as unsightly so calculate beforehand exact levels, rehanging doors if necessary.

Sheet vinyl is probably the most common and least expensive form of kitchen

floor covering and comes in a variety of different colors and patterns. Many of these can give very pleasing imitations of ceramic or even polished wooden floors. Vinyl lasts well, can be cleaned easily, is waterproof, and resistant to oils, fat, and most chemicals – though not to heat. It can be laid on hardboard, over floorboards, and can be cushioned underneath for greater warmth and comfort. Even cheaper than sheet vinyl, vinyl composition comes in the form of brittle tiles. A textured finish on vinyl shows fewer stains and is more slip-resistant.

Although vinyl flooring is extremely popular and practical, cork tiling is also

TERRACOTTA TILES

In the rustic kitchen of an old country house, the furniture is freestanding and old fashioned (below left) and the materials are natural. A floor of terracotta quarry tiles is the natural and traditional choice for such a room. Quarry tiles age beautifully, are durable, and highly attractive. However, traditional tiles of this kind are best used at ground-floor level and the subfloor must be carefully considered before you start work.

CHECKERBOARD CERAMIC

Elegant checkerboard squares, traditionally in ceramic tiles or stone, look good in most kitchens. Here (below right), the checkerboard design on the floor echoes the square tiles below the worksurface and on the walls. If a floor is not suitable for ceramic tiles, a similar effect can be easily achieved by using patterned vinyl flooring instead. This is relatively cheap and easy to maintain.

worth considering. It is an excellent insulator, for both sound and heat, and is pleasantly warm to walk on. Cork tiles are easy to clean, but may chip and dent.

Ceramic tiles look splendid, are long-lasting, and easy to clean. They can feel cold underfoot, however (this will depend in part on your heating arrangements), are expensive and, as mentioned, are not suitable for all types of floor. Terracotta tiles add visual as well as literal warmth underfoot.

Heavy-duty quarry tiles are extremely hard-wearing: they are non-slip and extremely tough, but the weight of them makes them impractical for a floor above

ground level, and upper floor kitchens are better off with good quality vinyl flooring. Terracotta, granite, and marble are also tough and durable, as are wooden floors, as long as they are heavily sealed in areas of constant use.

Linoleum, for many years regarded as old-fashioned and unattractive, is enjoying a revival, with some extremely good designs available. Sheet lineoleum is hardwearing, manufactured to industrial standards, and not difficult to lay, but it usually requires a hardboard sub-floor.

Wood is also worth considering for the kitchen, although it does absorb grease stains and requires regular scrubbing in

order to keep it clean. Painted floors are impractical, as are carpet and coir.

Whichever floor covering you choose, do not attempt to lay it yourself without advice either from the retailer or the manufacturer. Always check that the surface or sub-floor on which it is to be laid is correctly prepared and treated.

Make absolutely sure that you are using the right adhesive and the correct edging; that there is no dampness below the floor; and that you are equipped with precisely the right tools for the laying and trimming. If you are not confident, call in experts to lay the floor for you – this will be less expensive than re-doing it yourself.

DURABLE RUBBER

Synthetic rubber stud flooring is available in sheets or large tiles. Its appeal lies partly in its smart, contemporary appearance and partly in its excellent durability and ease of maintenance. The range of colors available makes it suitable for a wide variety of modern kitchen styles. Here (below left), bright red has been used to provide a splash of color in an otherwise completely white kitchen.

NATURAL CORK

Cork is a warm surface for a kitchen floor; it has the advantages of being a natural material which is easy on the eye, and is a relatively inexpensive alternative to wood. It is not as durable as vinyl or rubber, but ages pleasantly and, if properly sealed and polished, it is not difficult to maintain. In this neat and functional kitchen (below right), wall-to-wall cork tiling provides a perfect complement to the wooden table and chairs.

UTILITY ROOMS

A utility room should be functional, practical, and labor-saving, but it does not need to be a large room. It should have enough space for a washing machine and clothes dryer, a sink and drainer, storage cupboards, and a drying rack.

In a self-contained utility room, clothes can be washed, dried, and ironed, household cleaning equipment stored, and essential chores such as shoe cleaning and clothes mending performed. Dangerous materials such as bleach and cleaning fluids should always be kept out of reach of children, preferably in childproof wall-mounted closets.

Utility rooms need to be carefully planned and fitted, so consider first your sink, washer, and dryer; these should be positioned to allow easy access for repairs, servicing, and ventilation. A double sink with a generous draining board is particularly useful in a utility room, where clothes can be soaked, bleached, and washed by hand. Decide whether your existing plumbing system is adequate for your equipment. If not, call in professional help to make any necessary alterations. Remember that laundry equipment can leak occasionally, so the floor should be easy to clean.

If space in the utility room is limited, a drying rack can be suspended from the ceiling and an ironing board can even fold down from the wall.

An open utility area is hidden when not in use by a large Venetian blind (above). The ironing board folds out from a cupboard when needed.

A changing area for a baby, below a porthole window on to the garden, has been incorporated into this attractive utility room, created in a lean-to extension (below left).

Utility rooms can often be installed in narrow spaces (opposite and below right) where a line of units houses the machines and a sink. Use the space above for useful cabinets or shelves where dangerous cleaning materials can be safely stored out of children's reach.

DINING ROOMS

Today, eating rooms are frequently incorporated into the living room or kitchen. The short leg of an L-shaped living room or one corner or a wall of a kitchen often act as the eating room. The kitchen table itself is frequently where a family gathers to eat, and a separate dining room – with all the suggestions of formality that dining conveys – has become something of a rarity or luxury. A totally separate dining room is therefore something worth cherishing.

Traditionally, the formal dining room was a place of ostentatious and magnificent display. Carefully segregated from the kitchen, which was frequently a food-chilling distance off, it boasted suites of matching furniture in mahogany or walnut, on which gleamed the family silver. Above these, the walls were crowded with family portraits. Meals were served with a matching formality.

Recently the reaction to such formality, plus the fact that many homes do not have the space for a dining room proper, has obscured the real potential of dining rooms. An elegant but welcoming and attractive eating room is the perfect setting for relaxed, leisurely, sociable meals. Comfortable chairs and soft lighting encourage guests to linger, talking, over their food and wine; eating together is a supremely social act.

But a dining room can serve other functions besides just eating and entertaining, important though these two are. A desk in one corner can make it an extra room for quiet study, a comfortable armchair another place for reading.

The dining room is also a place for display, particularly if it is not in as frequent use as the other living areas. It can offer a place to exhibit treasured or "best" objects such as dishes, glasses, candlesticks, and racks of wine.

If you like, and can afford, antique or reproduction formal furniture such as mahogany sideboards, then your dining room style is set and you can enhance it best with beautifully finished shelves and a flattering lighting system. However, as an alternative, consider building a display unit or a fitted sideboard. Display crystal glasses on glass shelves, a china collection on open plate racks, or open a pass-through between the kitchen and dining room and make it a decorative feature.

Far from being outdated, an imaginatively planned dining room greatly enhances a home and your lifestyle.

DECORATIVE DISPLAYS

In a cool, sleek room the modern dining table and chairs are placed beside a wall of display shelving (opposite above). Here, books and music equipment are on show, but such a structure could be equally effective for storing china or glass.

A collection of ceramic pots is magnificently displayed in a dining room (below right) on shelves built into a false alcove. The pots are perfectly lit from a spotlight (not shown) placed above them.

An attractive unit (opposite below left) has been designed like a traditional dresser top. A larger unit (opposite below right) creates a fitted dresser, with a backing of wood paneling and drawers incorporated below a wide central shelf. With its gently mottled paint finish, it is the perfect background for a display of 1930s china.

DINING AREAS

An antique table and chairs are placed in a section of an open-plan layout (below left) to provide a formal dining room atmosphere. Note the attractive display shelves which are part of the adjoining kitchen and act as a screen.

In an old house, a creative modern design (opposite below center) incorporates a fitted metal table with window shelves.

KITCHEN SYSTEM

The problem faced by many people when trying to install a fitted kitchen is that most walls are out of true and uneven, and are often not at right angles to the floor. The whole process of installing your immaculate factory-made cabinets can easily become a nightmare, which is made worse when walls are covered with pipes and electrical wiring.

This system is designed to make the installation and scribing of kitchen fixtures as simple as possible; it allows existing pipework to run behind the fixtures and, most importantly, allows you to decide for yourself what sort of finish is most suited to your personal style.

This is a kitchen system that enables you to plan your space in the best possible way, allowing you to put all your cooking equipment on display or, if you prefer, shut away behind closed doors. You can incorporate gleaming new modern equipment, or use existing oven ranges and refrigerators. The dimensions are flexible and the permutations are innumerable.

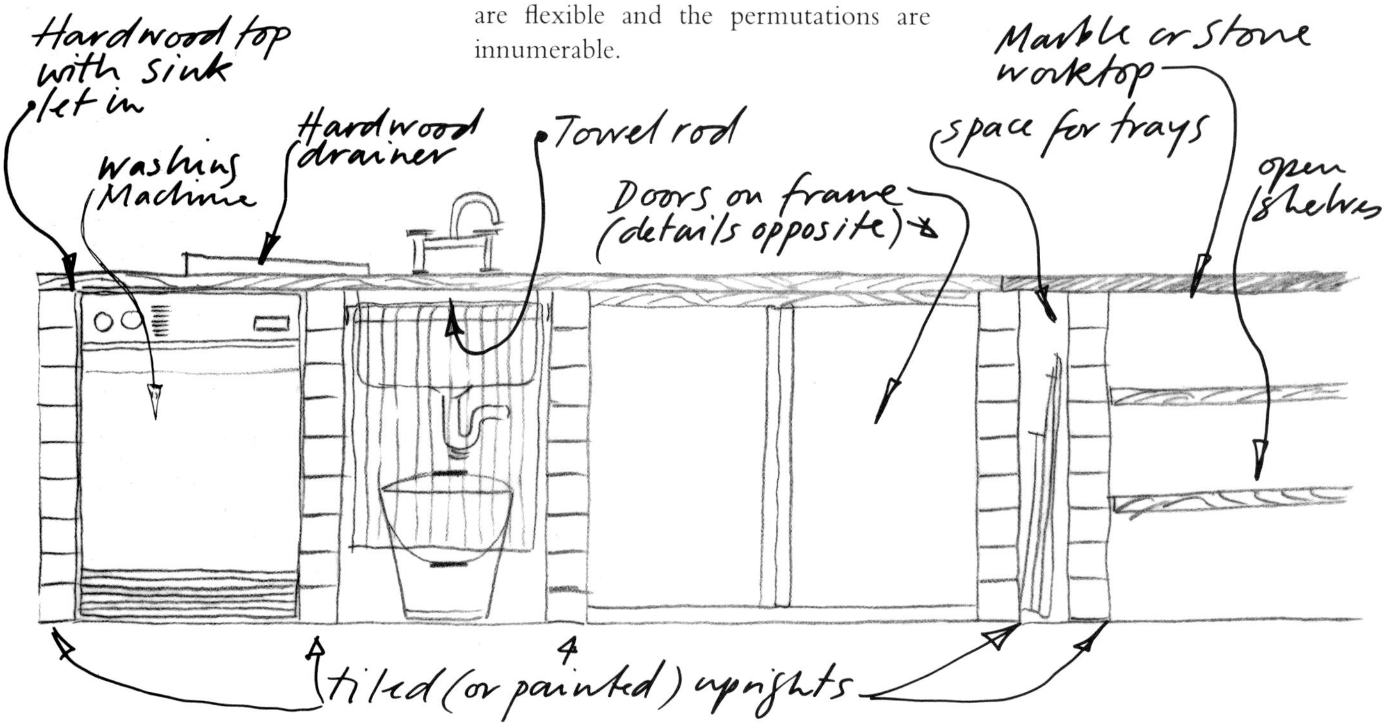

Hardwood top
with sink
let in

washing
Machine

Hardwood
drainer

Towel rod

Doors on frame
(details opposite) →

Marble or stone
worktop

space for trays

open
shelves

tiled (or painted) uprights

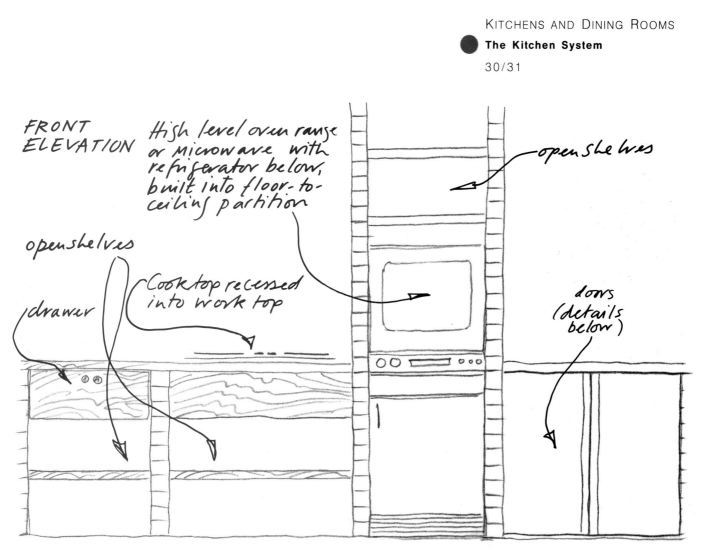

FRONT ELEVATION

High level oven range or microwave with refrigerator below, built into floor-to-ceiling partition

open shelves

open shelves

drawer

Cook top recessed into work top

doors (details below)

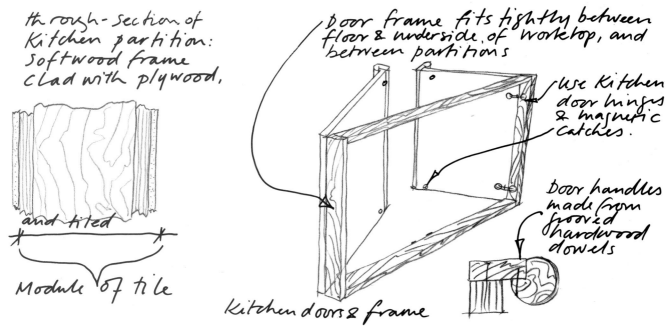

through-section of Kitchen partition: softwood frame clad with plywood,

and tiled

Module of tile

Door frame fits tightly between floor & underside of worktop, and between partitions

use Kitchen door hinges & magnetic catches.

Door handles made from grooved hardwood dowels

Kitchen doors & frame

PAINTED KITCHEN

THE KITCHEN SYSTEM: PAINTED KITCHEN

In this rustic kitchen, the basic partition units have been painted rather than tiled. Open shelves have been incorporated in between the partitions and a rod for hanging towels has been built-in underneath the sink. A wood edge-banded tiled worktop lies over the partition units and provides a workspace that is both practical and easy to clean.

To complete the country atmosphere, traditional slatted shelves, a hanging bar for kitchen utensils, and a knife rack have been mounted on the wall. These provide extra storage, are easy to construct, and make stylish additions to the basic kitchen system.

LAUNDRY ROOM

Using much the same basic system as the kitchen, the sturdy uprights of the laundry unit support a traditional deep-glazed ceramic Belfast sink which is set beneath a solid maple "butcher block" worktop. A washing machine and clothes dryer can be placed on floor plinths and are here housed on either side of the sink, underneath the worktop, to give a neat, symmetrical appearance.

A slatted shelf is built-in under the sink and between the two partition units to provide storage for laundry detergent and other essential cleaning materials. Below the shelf there is room for a large laundry basket for dirty clothes.

A drying rack on a pulley can be built and positioned over the unit for drying clothes, sheets, and large items such as duvets. With an area like this, doing the laundry could almost become a pleasure.

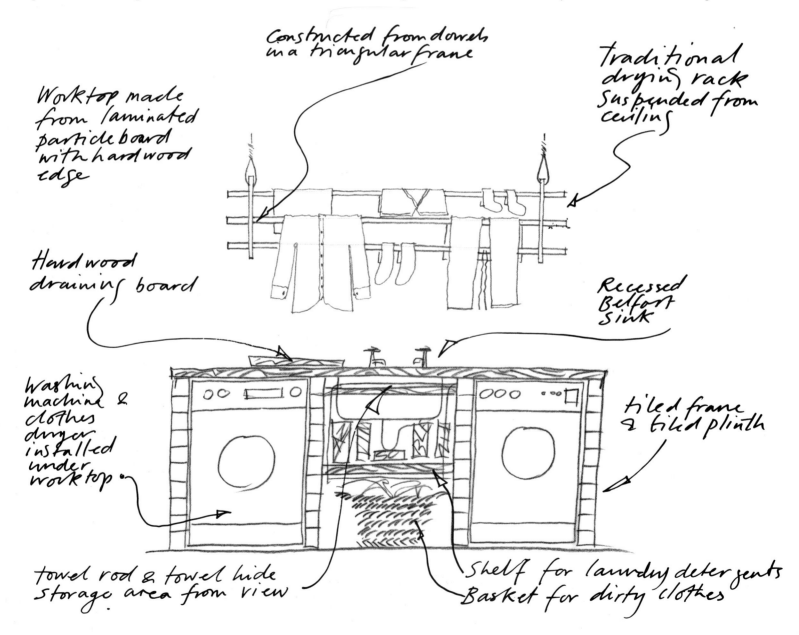

Constructed from dowels in a triangular frame

traditional drying rack suspended from ceiling

Worktop made from laminated particle board with hardwood edge

Hardwood draining board

Recessed Belfast sink

Washing machine & clothes dryer installed under worktop

tiled frame & tiled plinth

towel rod & towel hide storage area from view

Shelf for laundry detergents
Basket for dirty clothes

The Kitchen System

The basic element of this kitchen is the upright partition, which is tiled. Alternatively, it could be painted, clad in tongued, grooved, and V-jointed lumber, or covered with melamine or plastic laminate.

The width of the partition panels is adjusted to match the width of the tiles being used so that they exactly cover the edges of the tiles that are fixed to the sides of the panels. The spacing between the partitions is adjusted to suit the width of the appliances, shelves, and cupboards to be fitted. A worktop covers the tops of the panels, and overhangs them by $\frac{3}{4}$in (20mm). As the overall width of the worktop affects the front-to-back depth of the partition panels, it is important to decide on the worktop depth right at the beginning (see **Worktops, page 46**).

The upright partition panels are assembled, clad (skinned), tiled, grouted, and battened ready for fixing the shelves, before the partitions are fitted in place.

Base Units

When building base units of a critical thickness, you may find it difficult to obtain wood of exactly the required thickness. In this case, buy wood that is slightly oversized and plane it to the correct thickness.

Height You may have to modify slightly the height of the panels to suit the tiles you are using and the equipment to be fitted into the kitchen. The working height used in this project is $36\frac{1}{2}$in (930mm), which allows for a worktop thickness of $1\frac{1}{2}$in (40mm), while the overall height of the basic element – the upright partition panel – is 35in (890mm). This height is based on using whole tiles to cover the partition panel (eight tiles high).

Depth The front-to-back depth of the partition panel is $24\frac{3}{4}$in (630mm), which allows a $25\frac{1}{2}$in (650mm) deep worktop to overlap the panel by $\frac{3}{4}$in (20mm). If you buy a standard $23\frac{1}{2}$in (600mm) deep worktop you should reduce the partition panel depth to $22\frac{3}{4}$in (580mm).

At the back of the panel, the rear stud is inset by 2in (50mm) to allow for scribing, if required, for pipe and conduit runs. This space can also be used to provide ventilation for oven ranges and refrigerators. Gas appliances must have a separate flue. Allowance has been made in the design for a back panel and/or a door to be fitted, if required.

Spacing You can adjust the spacing between partition panels to suit appliances, your preferences for cupboard widths, and so on. Our panels are $23\frac{1}{2}$in (600mm) apart.

Shelves The design allows the top shelf to rest one tile's height down from the top of the partition panel and to line up with the tiled fascias. When hardwood edge-banding is added, the shelf finishes flush with the front edge of the partition.

Intermediate shelves are also in line with the fascia tiles, but are set half-a-tile back from the front edge. This looks neat and allows doors to be installed on the front if desired. (The top shelf is not included in this case.) All shelves rest on wooden battens, which are hidden by the front edge-banding on the shelves.

Floor plinths These are optional, but they give a neat finishing touch, and are useful if the floor is uneven. The underside of the plinths can be shimmed as necessary if the floor is uneven, and the front edge scribed to the floor before tiling (see **Techniques, page 94**). The plinths are made one tile height high.

The kitchen system has been designed to be adapted easily. Full instructions for building the kitchens illustrated on pages 32–3, 34–5, and 37 are given on the following pages.

If you decide to build the complete system, the order of work checklists (below) will help you to compile your own construction schedule.

The elements of each kitchen are listed below for ease of reference:

Tiled Kitchen

Basic Partition Unit and Shelves
Optional extras:
  Back panel
  Floor plinth
  Removable towel rail
  Built-in slatted shelf
  Doors and door handles
Worktop
Tall Partition Unit
Wall-Mounted Shelf Unit
Additional projects:
  Built-in plate rack and drip tray
  Hanging bar for kitchen utensils

Order of Work Checklist

Tiled base units incorporating shelves, back panels, and floor plinths, and a worktop.

1 Decide depth of worktop.
2 Decide height of worktop (to match tile height and equipment).
3 Decide on thickness of partition units (the thickness of the partition must match the tile width).
4 Decide on spacing of units, and whether you will incorporate shelves or built-in appliances such as a dishwasher.
5 Construct the basic frame unit, including tall partitions if required.
6 Decide on quantity and position of shelves.
7 Mark out position of shelf-support battens.
8 Attach intermediate cross rails.
9 Clad the frame in $\frac{3}{4}$in (19mm) plywood, using common nails.
10 Fit the back panel support battens.
11 Tile the sides of the partition units except for the back and the bottom rows of tiles (to allow room for scribing the partition unit to fit).
12 Make and attach the shelf-support battens.
13 Put partitions in place, adding any remaining tiles; scribe to fit if necessary, and secure to wall battens and floor with angle brackets.
14 Cut the back panel and slot it into place.
15 Make up and fit the shelves.
16 Make, tile, and fit the floor plinth.
17 Tile the front faces of the partition units.
18 Fit the worktop and any edge-banding.
19 Fit the door frame if required.
20 Construct wall-mounted shelf unit (with shelves if required).

Painted Kitchen

Basic Partition Unit
Knife Rack
Wall-mounted Slatted Shelves
Removable Towel Rail

Order of Work Checklist

Painted partition units with shelves, and a tiled worktop.

1 Decide depth of worktop.
2 Decide height of worktop.
3 Decide thickness of partition units.
4, **5**, **6**, **7**, **8** as tiled kitchen.
9 Clad the frame in $\frac{3}{4}$in (19mm) MDF, using finishing nails punched in $\frac{1}{16}$in (2mm) below the surface.
10 Make and attach the shelf-support battens.
11 Attach MDF fascia panel to front edge of each partition.
12 Attach partition units in place, supported by vertical battens and angle brackets, and paint as required.
13 Make up and fit the shelves.
14 Install and tile the worktop.

TOOLS

UTILITY KNIFE

STEEL BENCH RULE

TRY SQUARE

CARPENTER'S LEVEL

HAND SAW (or circular saw)

BACK SAW

DRILL (hand or power)

COUNTERSINK DRILL BIT

MASONRY DRILL BIT

HAMMER

NAILSET

SCREWDRIVER (Phillips or slotted, depending on type of screws used)

SANDING BLOCK and SANDING PAPER (or power finishing sander)

TWO C-CLAMPS

PAINTBRUSH $1\frac{1}{2}$in (38mm)

TILING TOOLS

TILE-SCORING TOOL

TILE CUTTER

ADHESIVE SPREADER

TILE SPACERS

GROUT SPREADER

ADDITIONAL TOOLS

POWER SABER SAW for cutting panels and installing sinks and cooktops

ROUTER or POWER CIRCULAR SAW for making cabinet handles

DOWELING JIG for jointing worktops

V-BLOCK to hold doweling for door handles

MATERIALS

Note: All lumber dimensions are finished sizes.
Materials listed are for constructing one base unit with shelves, and a floor plinth.

BASE UNIT – BASIC FRAME

Part	Quantity	Material	Length
FRONT STUD	1	2 × 3in (50 × 75mm) S4S softwood	35in (890mm)
BACK STUD	1	As above	32in (815mm)
TOP RAIL	1	As above	$23\frac{1}{4}$in (592mm)
BOTTOM RAIL	1	As above	$23\frac{1}{4}$in (592mm)
INTERMEDIATE RAILS	As required	As above	$21\frac{3}{4}$in (555mm)

CLADDING (covering for frame and floor)

SIDES	2	$\frac{3}{4}$in (19mm) water-resistant plywood	35 × $24\frac{3}{4}$in (890 × 630mm)
FLOOR	1	As above	$23\frac{1}{2}$ × $24\frac{3}{4}$in (600 × 630mm)

SHELVES

TOP SHELF	1	$\frac{5}{8}$in (15mm) plastic laminate particleboard	$23\frac{1}{2}$in (600mm) wide × $22\frac{3}{4}$in (575mm) deep
INTERMEDIATE SHELF	1	$\frac{5}{8}$in (15mm) plastic laminate particleboard	$23\frac{1}{2}$in (600mm) wide × $22\frac{3}{4}$in (575mm) deep
TOP AND INTERMEDIATE SHELF EDGE-BANDING		$\frac{1}{2}$ × $1\frac{1}{2}$in (12 × 38mm) planed hardwood	$23\frac{1}{2}$in (600mm)

SHELF-SUPPORT BATTENS

TOP SHELF	1	1 × 1in (25 × 25mm) S4S softwood	$24\frac{1}{2}$in (618mm)
INTERMEDIATE SHELF	1	As above	$22\frac{3}{4}$in (575mm)

FLOOR PLINTH

FRONT SUPPORT JOIST	1	1 × 4in (25 × 100mm) S4S softwood	$23\frac{1}{2}$in (600mm)
MIDDLE SUPPORT JOIST	1	As above	As above
REAR SUPPORT JOIST	1	As above	As above

TILES

TILES	As required	$4\frac{1}{4}$ × $4\frac{1}{4}$in (108 × 108mm) white ceramic wall and floor tiles	

BASIC FRAME

Nail the front stud to the top rail using 3in (75mm) 8d common nails. Make this job easier by nailing against a spare batten clamped to a bench, nailed to the floor, or fixed to a wall, so that there is something solid to nail against. Ideally, the parts will rest on a flat surface while they are being nailed to help hold them flush and keep them stable.

Turn the assembly over and nail the front stud to the bottom rail.

Nail the back stud between the top and bottom rails, 2in (50mm) in from the ends, and nail it in place. This will make it easier to fit the unit to the rear wall later on.

In the case of the partition panel for the laundry area, the back stud should be inset by 4in (100mm), which will allow for a ducting pipe from the clothes dryer.

POSITIONING THE INTERMEDIATE RAILS

Intermediate cross rails coincide with the center line of the shelf support positions, so these must be decided upon at this stage. The finished project will look better if the shelves align with joints between whole tiles. In our basic unit, one shelf is positioned one tile height down from the top, and the other is mid-way between this shelf and the surface of the floor plinth.

On the front and back studs, measure down and mark the shelf top at the required height. Next, mark off the shelf thickness of $\frac{5}{8}$in (15mm) and then the thickness of the shelf support batten, $\frac{3}{4}$in (19mm). The middle of the batten position will be the center line of the internal cross rail. Repeat the procedure for the second shelf.

With the basic square frame resting on edge (support the back stud with a waste piece of 2in [50mm] wood), nail the intermediate rails, correctly positioned, in place.

CLADDING THE FRAME

On the outside edges of the front and back studs, mark the center lines of the cross rails. The sides (which will be nailed to these cross rails) will conceal these rail positions. It is best to mark the center lines of the rails accurately, although the heads of the fixing nails give a rough guide to the positions of the cross rails. Also mark the center line of the back stud on the faces of the top and bottom rails of the frame.

Lay the frame flat, place a side panel cut from $\frac{3}{4}$in (19mm) water-resistant ACX plywood on top (A face uppermost), and align the front edge of the panel with the front edge of the front stud. If you are going to tile the panel, nail it in place *along the front edge only* using 4d common nails, about 6in (150mm) apart. If you are going to paint the panel, use MDF and finishing nails.

You will have made sure that the side panels are cut square, so use these as a guide to getting the basic frame square. Having nailed the front only, pull the rest of the frame into square, if necessary, to align with the edges of the panel, then nail through the panel into the frame, spacing the nails 6in (150mm) apart. To ensure that the nails go into the frame, transfer the center-line marks of the intermediate and back rails on to each side panel.

Turn the partition over and repeat for the other side panel.

TILING

It is best to tile the basic partition panels before they are installed, unless you include a back panel (*see* **Installing a Back Panel, page 42**). Lay the panel flat, mark guide lines to ensure accurate tile spacing, spread tile adhesive, and press the tiles in place, working on a small area at a time (*see* **Tiling Techniques, pages 94–5**). Tile from front to back and top to bottom.

If the floor or wall is uneven where the units are to stand (or if there are pipe runs to cover), leave off the back and bottom rows of tiles until the units have been scribed to fit (*see* **Techniques, page 91**). It is very important that the tiling lines up from one face of the pillar to another. Do not tile the front edge at this stage. When the tiles are dry, grout them. Turn over the units and repeat the process. Make up as many partition panels as you require.

① The Basic Frame
The back stud is inset by 2in (50mm) between the top and bottom rails to make scribing to the wall easier.

② First Intermediate Rail
Shelf batten position is one tile-height down from the top. Rail should coincide with position of the shelf.

③ Positioning Intermediate Rail for Lower Shelf
After the first intermediate rail has been nailed in place, the second one should be positioned accurately to coincide with the center line of the shelf-support batten.

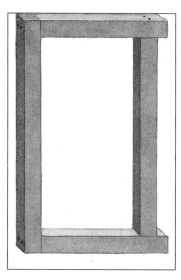

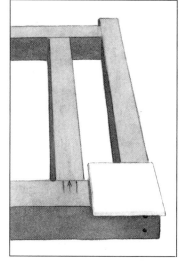

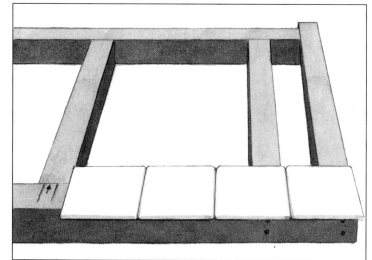

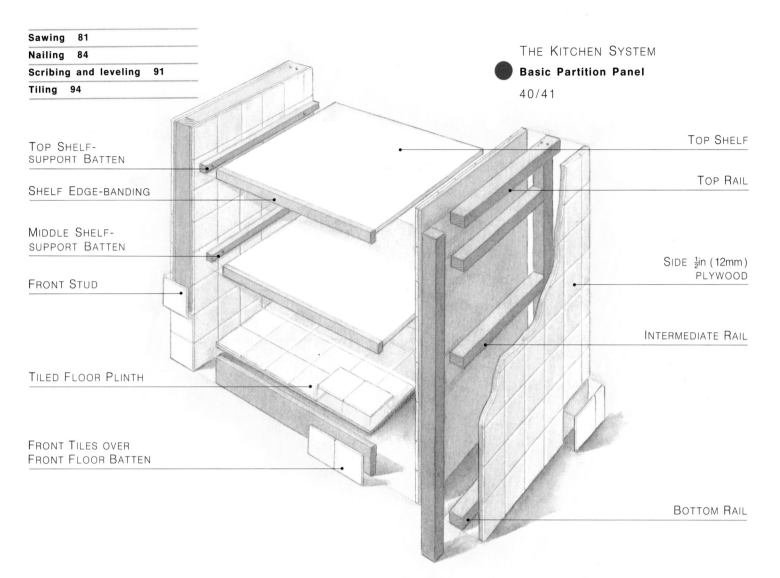

TOP SHELF-SUPPORT BATTEN

SHELF EDGE-BANDING

MIDDLE SHELF-SUPPORT BATTEN

FRONT STUD

TILED FLOOR PLINTH

FRONT TILES OVER FRONT FLOOR BATTEN

TOP SHELF

TOP RAIL

SIDE $\frac{1}{2}$in (12mm) PLYWOOD

INTERMEDIATE RAIL

BOTTOM RAIL

④ Cladding the Sides of the Basic Frame
Mark the center lines of the cross rails on the outside edges of the frames and carefully join up these marks on the $\frac{3}{4}$in (19mm) plywood as a guide for nailing the sides on to the frames.

⑤ Nailing Down the Side
Nail the front edges at 6in (150mm) intervals. Pull the frame square, then nail along the guide lines.

⑥ Tiling the Basic Partition
Tile from front to back and from top to bottom to keep cut tiles out of sight at the back or at floor level.

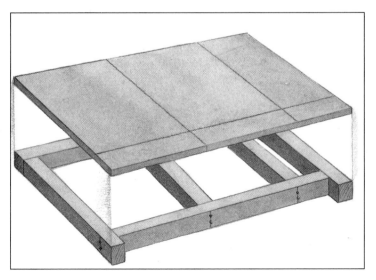

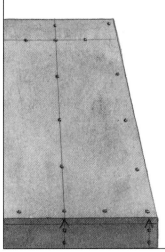

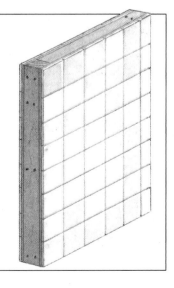

MAKING UP PARTITION UNITS

PAINTED PARTITION UNITS

Painted, as opposed to tiled, partition units are shown in the photograph on page 34, and illustrate the versatility of the basic unit design.

The building techniques are the same as before, except that the frames are clad in $\frac{3}{4}$in (19mm) MDF (medium-density fiberboard) instead of $\frac{3}{4}$in (19mm) plywood. For a smooth finish, carefully punch the finishing nail heads about $\frac{1}{16}$in (2mm) below the surface of the board, then fill the holes with a proprietary grain filler. The frame should be sanded down with a sanding block and sanding paper.

Finish the front edge of each partition unit by applying a strip of $\frac{1}{2}$in (12mm) MDF cut to the width of the frame and side panels. Nail in place and smooth in the same way as the side panels. Bevel the front edges of the fascia panels with a sanding block and add the shelf batten. Fit the panels in place (see opposite page) and paint them.

TALL PARTITION UNITS

Tall partition units are required to house eye-level wall ovens, microwave ovens, refrigerators, and so on. Construction is as for low partition units, fixing all the cross rails at the levels required to coincide with the supports. Remember to attach a rail where the worktop meets the partition as this will take a lot of weight.

As the maximum standard length of plywood is 8ft (2440mm) there will be a joint if the units are taller than this. The joint must be at a cross rail so that the cut edges can be nailed down. If there is not a convenient cross rail, then put in an extra one for this purpose.

SHELVES SUPPORTING OVEN RANGES

These shelves must be substantial, to support the weight of the appliance. Use 1×2in (25×50mm) battens for the shelf supports and 1in (25mm) particleboard or MDF for the shelves. The front fascia is cut from the same material, to the width of the shelf and to the height required – in this case, one tile deep. Either screw or glue and nail the front piece to the front edge of the shelf, and tile the front face.

INSTALLING A BACK PANEL

If a back panel is to be installed on a basic unit (perhaps to hide pipes where there is to be an open shelf), this must be done before installing the shelves and floor plinth, and also before tiling the sides. The front-to-back measurements of the shelves and floor should be reduced to make them fit. If the partition panel unit is to be installed over pipes, scribe the partition around these now to ensure a good fit (see **Techniques, page 91**).

Once all the partitions are sitting in place, correctly scribed, take the first partition and mark a line 2in (50mm) in from the back. Cut two lengths of 1×1in (25×25mm) batten to the height of the partition and attach a batten just in front of the marked line. Glue and nail it in position. Repeat for the second partition. Tile the surface (see **Techniques, page 94**), but only up to the batten. Repeat as necessary.

Make and screw on the shelf-support battens (see opposite page) allowing a $\frac{1}{4}$in (6mm) gap for the thickness of the back. Put partitions back in place and attach to the floor (see opposite page).

Cut the back panel from $\frac{1}{4}$in (6mm) MDF or plywood. The height is the same as the partitions, and the width is as the floor and shelf widths. Slot the panel in place from the top and screw through to the battens using four screws on each side. You may need to undo the shelf-support battens temporarily for an easy fit.

Make up the shelves (see opposite page), adjusting the front-to-back dimension accordingly. Replace the shelf-support battens and fit the shelves.

FLOOR PLINTHS

Each floor plinth is made from $\frac{1}{2}$in (12mm) water-resistant plywood with 1×4in (25×100mm) lumber joists supporting it, assuming you

---

1 Cladding Painted Partition Units
Use $\frac{3}{4}$in (19mm) MDF to clad units. Punch nail heads below surface.

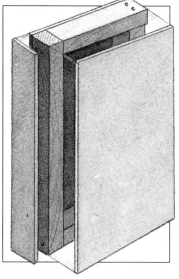

2 Construction of Tall Partition Units
The basic construction method is the same as for the low partition units. Intermediate rails should be included wherever shelves are required or attachments are to be made.

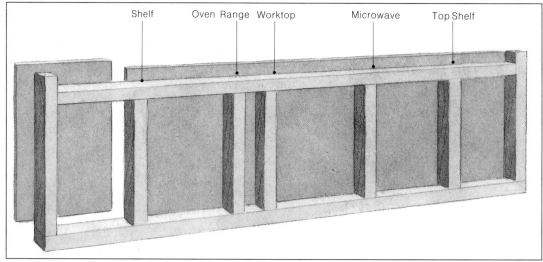

Shelf   Oven Range   Worktop   Microwave   Top Shelf

are using $4\frac{1}{4} \times 4\frac{1}{4}$in (108 × 108mm) tiles. The front-to-back dimensions are again adjusted accordingly.

Cut the $\frac{1}{2}$in (12mm) plywood plinth panel to size and nail the joists to it at the front, back, and middle. Inset the back one slightly to make scribing easier.

In a utility room or kitchen it is normal to set the washing machine and clothes dryer on the floor, but "built-in" models are also available, and these look better when set on tiled floor plinths as shown in the photograph. If you intend to do this, put in two extra support joists beneath the floor plinth to take the weight of the machines. Pack fiberglass batten insulation quilt between the joists to reduce the noise.

Tile the top from front to back and from the middle outwards, so that any cut tiles are equal at either side (see **Tiling Techniques, page 94**). Grout the tiles to finish. If an appliance is to be placed on a floor plinth, make sure that tiles suitable for floors and walls are chosen as thin wall tiles will crack under the weight and vibration.

SHELVES

We chose easy-to-clean plastic laminated particleboard for our shelves, but you may prefer to use another type of manmade board, such as lumber core or plywood (see **Materials, lumber and boards, page 76**). All shelves are edged at the front with a wooden edge-banding and this thickness has to be allowed for when fitting the shelf-support battens.

ATTACHING THE SHELF-SUPPORT BATTENS

The positions of the shelf supports are already marked on the front and back studs (see **Positioning Intermediate Rails, page 40**). With a pencil, connect the lines on the tiles.

Use 1 × 1in (25 × 25mm) S4S for the shelf supports, and cut them to the length required. The top one is the depth of the partition unit, minus the thickness of the edge-banding. The middle one is the partition depth, less half a tile height and the thickness of the edge-banding.

Hold each batten in position on the panel and mark two fixing-screw positions, approximately 2in (50mm) from the ends of each batten, but adjusted so that the screws will not be too near the edge of the tiles.

Using a $\frac{3}{16}$in (4.5mm) drill bit, drill two clearance holes in each batten. Hold each batten in place again and mark the screw positions on the tiles. Drill the tiles with a $\frac{9}{32}$in (7mm) masonry drill (see **Techniques, page 83**) to ensure that the batten-fixing screws will not crack the tiles when they are driven home.

Drill a $\frac{1}{8}$in (3mm) hole through the center of each clearance hole in the partition panel side. Countersink holes in the face of each batten and screw the battens into place using 2in (50mm) No 8 screws. Hide the battens by painting them a suitable color to blend with the tiles you have chosen.

MAKING THE SHELVES

Hold the shelf piece in a vise with the front edge, which is non-laminated, facing upwards.

Glue and nail $\frac{1}{2} \times 1\frac{1}{2}$in (12 × 38mm) planed wood edge-banding to this edge so that the top edge is flush. The edge-banding must underhang the shelf enough to hide the battens, that is by $\frac{3}{4}$in (19mm). Use 2d finishing nails, blunting the points first so as not to split the wood (see **Techniques, page 84**). Nail carefully, making sure the edge-banding is flush with the surface as you go. Wipe off surplus glue. Punch the nail heads below the surface, then fill the holes and sand down.

Paint, or stain and varnish, the edge-banding. Ours is stained with white oil to match the worktop.

Where a shelf has to fit into a corner, cut off the underhang of the edge-banding where the front of the shelf meets a partition, and screw a batten to the wall, level with the side battens of the partition unit, to support the shelf at the back.

INSTALLING PARTITION UNITS

The partition units are neatly secured to the rear wall with metal angle brackets at positions where

❸ **Fitting a Back Panel**
Scribe partition units around pipes and cut slots. Fit a panel-support batten to the face of the unit.

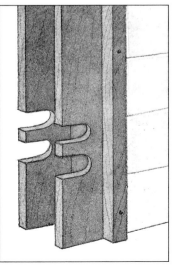

❹ **Construction of a Tiled Floor Plinth**
Floor plinth comprises $\frac{3}{4}$in (19mm) plywood on 1 × 4in (25 × 100mm) S4S lumber battens. The back batten is inset by about 2in (50mm). Front tiles overlap the edges of the top tiles.

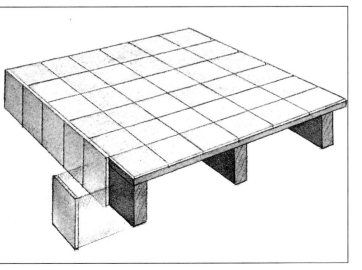

❺ **Fixing Shelves in Place**
Hardwood edge-banding attached to the front edge of a shelf (inset) hides support battens screwed to units.

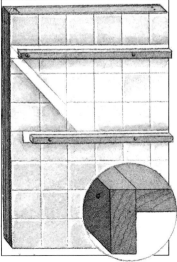

Cupboard Doors and Slatted Shelf

they will be hidden, at the very top and at shelf height. The units are also fitted to the floor with brackets which will be hidden by the floor plinth units when in place.

Position the partition units according to the plans. It is important to have a partition unit where you have to turn a corner, to support the two edges of the worktop.

Do any scribing necessary to secure the partitions to the wall or floor *(see* **Techniques, page 91** *).*

Where the partition unit is to be installed, screw a vertical batten to the wall. Finish tiling, then push the unit into place over the wall batten and screw it to the batten. Attach the shelves and floor plinth.

Secure the partition to the floor using angle brackets *(see* page 85 *).* Do this by removing the floor plinth and attaching the brackets where they will avoid the joists supporting the floor plinth. Slide the floor plinth back into position.

Fit high partitions to the wall batten, and to the floor and ceiling, if necessary, using angle brackets where they cannot be seen, such as

behind the oven range, just underneath the back shelf, or on top of the shelf above eye-level.

When all the partition units are installed, tile and grout their front faces to finish the units.

Doors

Doors are hinged in pairs and inset within a lumber frame as a neat addition to the basic unit.

Making the Frame

Measure the opening where the doors are to fit and make a frame to these external dimensions.

Dowel joint the horizontal rails between the uprights with two $\frac{1}{2}$in (12mm) dowels at each frame corner *(see* **Techniques, page 90** *).* While the glue is setting, the frame should be held square on a flat surface with bar clamps. Alternatively, you can improvise a clamp by resting the frame against a batten temporarily nailed to the bench top. Another batten is nailed to the bench a short distance from the other side of the frame, and then the

clamp is tightened by driving folding wedges *(see* **Techniques, page 81** *)* between the edge of the second batten and the frame side.

From $\frac{1}{2}$in (12mm) hardwood doweling cut eight dowels, the length of which should be twice the thickness of the wood it is going through, plus $\frac{1}{2}$in (12mm). Use a back saw to cut two grooves, $\frac{1}{32}$–$\frac{1}{16}$in (1–2mm) deep, along the dowel length. This will allow the glue and air to escape as the dowel is driven in. With sanding paper, round off one end of each dowel.

With a $\frac{1}{2}$in (12mm) drill bit, drill two holes through each corner joint to a depth of twice the thickness of the wood being fixed. Wrap a band of adhesive tape around the drill bit to indicate the correct depth.

Apply glue to each hole and wipe it around the inside with a small stick. Insert the dowels and hammer them almost home, leaving the ends protruding for the time being. Leave the frames clamped square.

When the glue has set, remove the clamps and saw off the dowel ends flush with the surface.

Installing the Frame

Before installing the frame, it must be held square by nailing a batten temporarily across the top and one side of the frame *(see* **Techniques, 3-4-5 method of bracing, page 80** and fig 2 below *).* After attaching the bracing batten, saw off the ends of the batten flush with the frame to make a neat edge.

Drill and countersink the uprights of the frame and the top and bottom rails. Put the frame in position and screw it to the partition units and to the floor. After fitting, remove the bracing batten from the frame.

Making the Doors

For a painted finish, cut the doors from $\frac{3}{4}$in (19mm) MDF so that they fit inside the frame with a $\frac{1}{16}$in (2mm) gap all around. There are many different types of door handles which can be fitted to finished doors. Below you will find instructions for making and fitting the handles shown in the illustration. Hinges and catches must also be fitted *(see* **Techniques, page 92** *).*

① Jointing of Frame Corners
Two $\frac{1}{2}$in (12mm) dowel holes in the ends of the rails are the same length as the thickness of the uprights.

② Making the Door Frame Square
Before fitting the frame, hold it square temporarily by nailing a batten across the top and one side using the 3-4-5 method of ensuring a right-angled corner (see Techniques, page 80 for further details).

③ Attaching Door Handles
A right-angled rabbet is cut in 1in (25mm) dowel which is attached to hardwood lipping on the door edge.

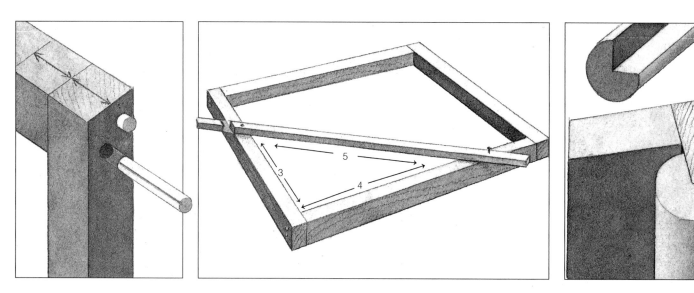

MAKING THE HANDLES

To make our handles you will need a router, and a V-block to hold the doweling from which the handles are made (see **Techniques, Making a V-block, page 83**). The doweling is placed in the V-block and rabbeted with the router. (You can use a circular saw for this, but it is much more difficult to achieve a good finish.) Cut the doors narrower by the thickness of the lipping, that is, $\frac{1}{2}$in (12mm).

Cut two lengths of 1in (25mm) diameter doweling, to the length of the door plus 2in (50mm) extra to allow the doweling to be nailed in the V-block. The V-block should be a 39in (1000mm) length of 2×3in (50×75mm) lumber with a 1in (25mm) deep V cut in one face. Nail each end of the dowel in the V-block and mark the finished length. Hold the V-block firmly in a vise.

Working from one end to the other, rout to the depth of the lipping ($\frac{1}{2}$in [12mm]) between the marks. Cut the dowel to final length. Cut two lengths of $\frac{1}{2} \times 1\frac{1}{4}$in ($12 \times 32$mm) hardwood lipping to the length of the dowels. Glue and nail the lipping to the dowel, then sand smooth. Glue and nail the lipping on to the door edges and finish as required.

SLATTED SHELF

Slatted shelves are easy to build and are particularly useful in airing cupboards. In the laundry room (see page 37) a slatted shelf has been built-in under the Belfast sink. A number of cross slats are nailed to side rails which rest alongside the same type of shelf-support battens as those used in the basic partition unit in the tiled kitchen.

Cut two pieces of 1×2in (25×50mm) planed lumber for the side rails to the required front-to-back depth of the shelf. Our shelf is set back about 4in (100mm). Cut the support battens to the same

HINGED DOOR ASSEMBLY
Doors are hinged within a simple frame assembly which is screwed between partition units.

length and attach in place (see **Shelf-Support Battens, page 43**).

Cut the required number of slats (we used seven) from the 1×2in (25×50mm) planed lumber. The length of these should be the width between partitions, less $\frac{1}{16}$in (2mm) to fit exactly.

Set the side rails in from the ends of the slats by the thickness of the supporting battens. Use offcuts or scrap wood of the same thickness as the support battens. Lay them next to the side rails before laying the front slat across them, so that the battens are at the very ends. Nail the slat in place.

Cut a spacing batten (see **Techniques, page 80**) to ensure that the remaining slats are spaced evenly, then nail them in place. Finish the shelf by painting, staining, or varnishing it as required.

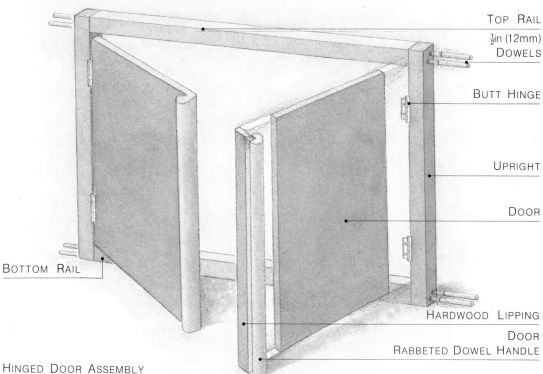

TOP RAIL
$\frac{1}{2}$in (12mm) DOWELS
BUTT HINGE
UPRIGHT
DOOR
HARDWOOD LIPPING
DOOR RABBETED DOWEL HANDLE
BOTTOM RAIL

④ Making a Slatted Under-sink Storage Shelf
A number of cross rails are nailed to side rails; these rails rest on 1×1in (25×25mm) shelf-support battens which are then secured at each side to the tiled partition units.

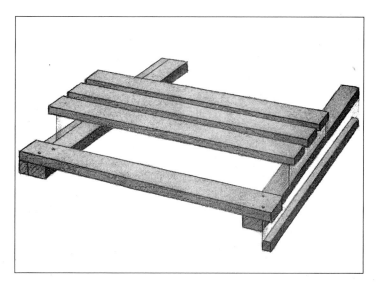

WORKTOPS

There is a wide range of worktops from which to choose. In the tiled kitchen we used 1½in (40mm) thick solid wood, finished with white oil. The worktop in the painted kitchen is 1in (25mm) particleboard which is tiled, and edge-banded at the front with hardwood. A wide selection of laminated worktops is available. The front edges are often rounded (post-formed), or they can be square-edged and edge-banded with hardwood. Most of these worktops are 1¼in (32mm) thick.

If a material like marble or granite is chosen, it will look better if it is made to look thicker at the front edge by bonding a strip of similar material under the front edge. At the back, the worktop's edge will probably be covered by the wall tiles.

Alternatively, the worktop can be attached to the wall by scribing, or by cutting into the wall, although it is easier to cover the gap at the back with a narrow hardwood strip fitted to the wall. If the wall is very uneven, a hardwood strip can be fitted horizontally to the back of the worktop. This strip can be scribed to the wall.

JOINING WORKTOPS

You will probably not need to join worktops end-to-end unless you have a very long run, but you will almost certainly need to turn a corner. Remember that all joins must coincide with a partition.

Joints should be doweled (see **Techniques, page 90**) using a doweling jig to ensure that the surfaces are absolutely flush. You then rout out or drill the surfaces for jointing connector bolts on the underside; there are several types available and they all come with fitting instructions. Alternatively, for corner jointing post-formed worktops, specially shaped metal strips are available to cover the joints neatly.

SECURING WORKTOPS

Fit the worktop to the partitions with knock-down angle plates – two per side of each partition – and screw up through any door frames into the worktop. If you are installing a solid-wood worktop, allow for expansion and shrinkage in the wood by using specially slotted angle plates. Where

a worktop meets a high partition, screw a 2 x 2in (50 x 50mm) batten to the partition for the worktop to rest on. Screw up into the worktop from the underside of the batten (if it is a solid wood worktop, use a slot screw). Angle the front edge of the support batten backwards and set it back from the front edge so it will not be seen. Another method of fitting a worktop is to use a flat metal plate screwed down into the pillar before the worktop is laid over it, and then up into the worktop (fig 2).

If the worktop is to be tiled, do this after fitting, then add a hardwood edge-banding. Seal the gap at the back of the worktop to finish.

SINKS AND COOKTOPS

These are supplied with templates for the required cut-outs. Hold the templates in position and draw around them. Drill ½in (12mm) diameter holes in each corner, inside the line. Put the blade of the Saber saw through one of the holes, and saw around the lines (see **Techniques, Cutting a circle, page 82**).

FRONT CONTROL PANEL FOR COOKTOP

Screw a small length of 1 x 1in (25 x 25mm) batten into the partitions at a depth and distance back to suit your control panel. Screw into the battens following the appliance manufacturer's instruction.

BELFAST SINK

This type of sink sits on a support under a cut-out in the worktop. Make a template of the inside shape of the sink and use this to make the cut-out (see **Sinks and Cooktops, left**). Because the worktop should overhang the sink, the cut-out must therefore be smaller than the inside of the sink. With a router, form a shallow groove on the underside of the worktop, all around the cut-out, about ¼in (6mm) from the edge. This is a drip groove, which will help to prevent water from running under the worktop. Seal around the rim of the sink and the underside of the worktop using silicone-rubber caulking. Make a circular cut-out in the shelf support to allow the waste

❶ How to Join Worktops
When joining worktops, reinforce the under-surface by fitting jointing connector bolts.

❷ Fixing Down Worktops
Angle plates (brackets) at top and corner plates at bottom are used for fixing worktops in place.

❸ Fitting of Inset Sink or Cooktop
Templates are supplied for marking the top so that a cut-out can be made with a Saber saw. Clips on the underside of the sink or cooktop hold the appliance in place once a hole has been cut.

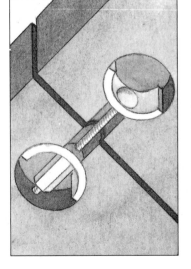

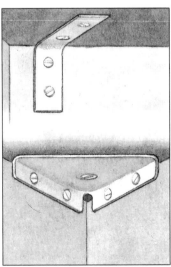

trap to be fitted into the sink. Stiffen the front edge of the shelf support with 1 × 2in (25 × 50mm) wood edge-banding. Cut a hole, or holes, in the worktop behind the sink to allow the taps to be fitted. Belfast sinks are very heavy, so it may be wise to consult a plumber before attempting to install one yourself.

TILING A WORKTOP

Tiling a worktop provides a very hard-wearing, hygienic surface which is easy to clean and therefore ideal for a kitchen. However, a tiled surface is not suitable for all purposes – for food preparation you need a smooth, wipe-clean surface, such as plastic laminate. For chopping vegetables and meat you need a surface of solid hardwood, such as maple, which is what butchers' blocks are made from. So in a kitchen there is a good case for having a choice of worksurfaces.

When buying tiles for a worktop, be sure to tell your supplier what you will be using them for. Some thin wall tiles will crack when used to work on,

so thicker tiles suitable for both walls and floors are preferable. Some outdoor-type tiles, particularly those with a metallic glaze, are not suitable as a surface for food preparation.

If possible, avoid white grout as it is very difficult to keep clean, although the latest two-part epoxy type is better in this respect. A good choice is a dark-colored waterproof grout. A wide range of colored grouts is available, and coloring powders can be mixed with white grout to your own requirements. If tiles without spacers are used, keep them close together to minimize the width of grouting.

It is essential that the worksurface to be tiled is stable and securely attached before you begin tiling. We recommend 1in (25mm) particleboard. Plywood of the same thickness is also suitable, although more expensive. Try to avoid tiling over solid wood as the wood tends to expand and shrink too much, thus loosening the tiles.

Before starting to tile, tack a batten temporarily to the outer edge of the worktop to give a surface to

tile against. Then lay out the tiles in a dry run to see whether any cutting will be required. This will almost certainly be the case, so keep the cut tiles to the back. If the tiles have to be cut at each end of the worksurface, make sure that the cut ones will be at least half a tile's width. If the initial laying out reveals only thin strips at each end, move all of the tiles sideways by half a tile's width so as to make the end tiles wider.

On the temporary edging batten, mark where the middle tile falls and start tiling from there. Spread tile adhesive over the worktop to cover about 1yd square (1m square) using a notched tile adhesive spreader to ensure an even bed of adhesive. Press the middle tile into the adhesive with a slight twisting motion, then add other tiles to the front edge on each side of this tile. Make sure that they butt against the temporary edging batten. Next, fit whole tiles, working back from the front middle tile towards the back wall. Use a try square and a straight-edge to ensure that this row is straight. Now, working from front to

back again, fill in with tiles on each side of this row to complete the main area of tiling. After this, cut and fit the edge tiles (see **Tiling Techniques, page 94**).

Complete the job by removing the temporary edging batten and replacing it with hardwood edge-banding, the top edge of which should be level with the surface of the tiles. The edge-banding should be deep enough to cover the entire thickness of the worktop. Grout the joints between the tiles and the space between the tiles and the edge-banding. Finally, seal the tile-to-wall joint with silicone-rubber caulking to make it waterproof.

④ Working out Tile Positions
Tack a batten temporarily to the front edge of the worktop. Set out tiles in a "dummy run."

⑤ Order for Laying Tiles
Lay front tiles from the middle, then work to the back and fill in at each side of the worktop.

⑥ Tiled Worktop
In the painted kitchen shown on page 34, our tiled worktop is finished off with a neat wooden edge-banding to create a functional but attractive surface to work on when preparing food.

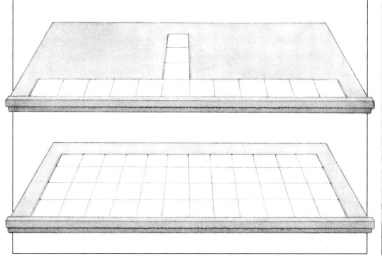

WALL-MOUNTED SHELF UNIT

The wall-mounted shelf units are built in a similar way to the floor units. They are neatly mounted to wall battens, so there is no visible means of support. When the units are mounted on a stud wall, extra support is required and so horizontal battens are secured to the wall to support the vertical wall battens. Therefore, the top and bottom rails are thinner in these units, and the sides have cut-outs at the back to slot over the battens on the wall.

MAKING THE PARTITION

Remember that each shelf unit needs a partition panel at each end. Some partitions will support shelving at each side.

Mark out on the walls where you want the shelf runs to be. For the best visual effect, keep the wall shelf partitions above the center lines of the base partitions. Work out what you want to incorporate within the shelves – for example, a stove hood, a plate rack, and a hanging bar for utensils. Decide on the overall height of the shelving. In our case, the partitions are $23\frac{1}{2}$in (600mm) high by $13\frac{3}{4}$in (350mm) deep.

The basic frame is made from 2×2in (50×50mm) S4S (smooth 4 sides) lumber clad with $\frac{1}{4}$in (6mm) MDF (medium-density fiberboard) panels. Two panels are required for each partition unit.

Cut two rails (for top and bottom) $13\frac{3}{4}$in (350mm) long, and three uprights 20in (510mm) long. Note that for attaching to a stud (hollow) wall, the top and bottom rails will be 1×2in (25×50mm) and $12\frac{3}{4}$in (325mm) long.

Nail together the basic frame so that the back stud is set one stud's thickness in. Glue and nail on the side panels, fixing one edge first, before pulling the frame into square so that the other sides line up with the panel. Check that the wall batten slides into the back space.

TOOLS

UTILITY KNIFE

STEEL BENCH RULE

TRY SQUARE

HAMMER

NAILSET

HAND SAW (or circular power saw)

BACK SAW

SCREWDRIVER

SANDING BLOCK and SANDING PAPER (or power finishing sander)

DRILL (hand or power)

DRILL BITS

COUNTERSINK BIT

MASONRY DRILL BIT

PLANE

CARPENTER'S LEVEL

PAINTBRUSH

ADDITIONAL TOOLS

METAL or STUD DETECTOR

SPADE DRILL BIT for drilling partition units for hanging bar

MATERIALS

Part	Quantity	Material	Length
PARTITION UNIT (two required per shelf)			
SIDE PANEL	2	$\frac{1}{4}$in (6mm) MDF	$13\frac{3}{4} \times 23\frac{1}{2}$in ($350 \times 600$mm)
FRONT FASCIA PANEL	1	$\frac{1}{4}$in (6mm) MDF	As above
TOP RAIL*	1	2×2in (50×50mm) S4S lumber	$13\frac{3}{4}$in (350mm)
BOTTOM RAIL*	1	As above	As above
FRONT STUD	1	As above	20in (510mm)
BACK STUD	1	As above	As above
WALL BATTEN	1	As above	As above
SHELVES			
TOP SHELF	1	$\frac{5}{8}$in (15mm) plastic laminate particleboard	$12\frac{3}{4} \times 23\frac{1}{2}$in ($325 \times 600$mm), or as required
BOTTOM SHELF	1	As above	As above
MIDDLE SHELF	1	$\frac{5}{8}$in (15mm) plastic laminate particleboard	$10 \times 23\frac{1}{2}$in (250×600mm), or as required
SHELF EDGE-BANDING	3	$\frac{1}{2} \times 1\frac{1}{2}$in ($12 \times 38$mm) hardwood	As above
TOP AND BOTTOM SHELF SUPPORT BATTENS	4	1×1in (25×25mm) S4S lumber (plane one face down to $\frac{5}{8}$in [15mm])	$12\frac{3}{4}$in (325mm)
MIDDLE SHELF SUPPORTS	2	As above	10in (250mm)
*TOP RAIL (for stud wall fixing)	1	1×2in (25×50mm) S4S lumber	$12\frac{3}{4}$in (325mm)
*BOTTOM RAIL (for stud wall fixing)	1	As above	As above

TOP SHELF-SUPPORT BATTEN

SHELF EDGE-BANDING

MIDDLE SHELF-SUPPORT BATTEN

MIDDLE SHELF

BOTTOM SHELF-SUPPORT BATTEN

BOTTOM SHELF

FRONT FASCIA PANEL

TOP SHELF

WALL BATTEN

BACK STUD

FRONT STUD

BOTTOM RAIL

① The Partition Basic Frame
Note that the back stud is inset by the thickness of the wall batten for a neat fit and to make scribing easier.

② Cladding the Frame Unit
$\frac{1}{4}$in (6mm) MDF is nailed to the sides, and front fascia is nailed on to cover the edges of the frame unit.

③ Attaching Shelf Battens
Battens are positioned at the top, middle, and bottom. *Inset*: attaching a batten to make the top flush.

④ Solid Wall Fixing Method
Batten is securely anchored and screwed to the wall; the partition (cut-away) slots over the batten.

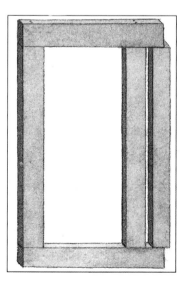

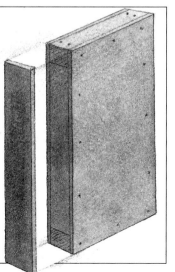

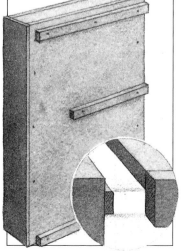

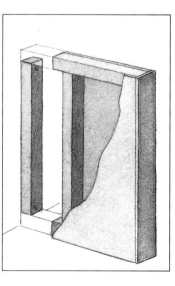

WALL-MOUNTED SHELF UNIT

Measure the total thickness of the partition and cut front fascia strips from $\frac{1}{4}$in (6mm) MDF to that width and $23\frac{1}{2}$in (600mm) high.

Nail on the front fascia and punch the nail heads below the surface (*see* **Techniques, page 84**). Bevel the edges with a plane and sand them down. If the panels are to be a different color from the wall, it is a good idea to paint them before you secure them to the wall.

SHELF-SUPPORT BATTENS

Plane the lumber down to $\frac{5}{8} \times 1$in (15×25mm) to make shelf support battens, and fit these to the partitions before fixing the partitions to the wall. The shelves will look better if they are set back slightly from the front of the partitions. The middle shelf has to be set back even farther – about 4in (100mm).

Decide how many shelves you need and where you want them according to your storage requirements. Ours are flush with the top and bottom of the partitions, with a middle shelf midway between the top and bottom shelves.

1 **Stud Wall Fixing Method**
The wall batten is screwed to horizontal battens that are nailed to wall studs.

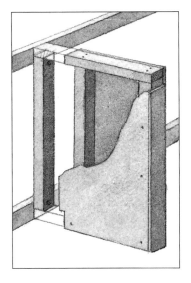

Cut the support battens to length, allowing for the edge-banding which is nailed to the front edge of the shelf (that is, the battens are cut to the shelf's depth). Glue, then screw or nail the battens in place.

SHELVES

The shelves are made from $\frac{5}{8}$in (15mm) plastic laminate particle-board with $\frac{1}{2}$in (12mm) hardwood edge-banding. Glue and nail the edge-banding to the front edge. Fill the nail holes, sand smooth when dry and finish according to your decorative scheme.

PLATE RACK

If you are incorporating a plate rack (see opposite page for assembly instructions), it is important to make this up before securing in place the supporting partitions which stand on either side of it.

INSTALLING THE PARTITIONS

Solid walls In most cases the partitions will be secured above a worktop. This should have been fitted level, so measure up from it when marking the positions of the wall battens. Use a carpenter's level to double check that these marks are level. Then, using masonry nails, temporarily fix a straight horizontal batten to the wall on which the wall battens rest while they are fixed. Drill the wall for anchors and screw the wall battens securely to the wall.

Slot the partition unit over the wall battens and glue and screw through the sides into the wall battens with 1in (25mm) No 8 woodscrews, using four either side.

Stud walls Locate the wall studs (*see* **Techniques, Wall fixtures, page 85**) and nail a 2×2in (50×50mm) batten horizontally at the top and bottom of where the partition units will be placed. Screw the 2×2in (50×50mm) upright wall battens to the horizontal battens on the wall for support.

Nail up the frame as before, but use 1×2in (25×50mm) lumber for the top and bottom rails which will be shorter by the thickness of the horizontal battens. Cut out 1×2in (25×50mm) slots on the back corners of the inside panels using a 1×2in (25×50mm) lumber offcut as a template. Nail the panels down, then slot the partitions over the wall battens, screwing through the sides into the wall battens as before. Do not include cut-outs at the ends of the shelf units.

STOVE HOOD

This hood can be the simple recirculating type, which needs only to be attached between two partition panels and connected to a power supply, or it can be the more efficient extractor type. With the latter, you will

USE SHELVES FOR DISPLAY
The wall-mounted shelf unit is ideal for decorative display as well as for practical storage.

need to cut an outlet in a convenient external wall for fumes to escape through. The hood is then either connected directly to the outlet or linked to it with simple slot-together plastic ducting if they are some distance apart. The manufacturer's instructions will have full details.

It will probably be necessary to attach mounting battens to both the wall and the partition units. Fit a narrow shelf at the top to line up with the top of the partition units, but do not fit edge-banding at the front as the stove hood's front panel will conceal this. Attach battens at an angle on each inside face of the partition units to hold the front panel. This can be a sheet of stainless steel or painted MDF. If you use MDF, secure the panel by screwing through into the battens. But if the panel is stainless steel, it is neater to glue it in place with epoxy resin.

You can adapt the fitting of the stove hood according to its design and how it fits into the rest of your kitchen system.

HANGING BAR FOR UTENSILS

This is simply a chrome steel or wooden rod which fits at each end into a wall partition panel. S-shaped meat hooks are hung on the bar to take utensils.

To install the bar, drill holes of its diameter into the sides of the appropriate partition unit so that the bar will clear the bottom rail but will rest on it. Use an offcut of bottom rail as a spacer to mark off the lowest part of the hole on the bottom edge of the partition panel.

Cut the rod to a length equivalent to the distance between two partition panels, plus 4in (100mm).

2 Positioning the Hanging Bar
Use an offcut of the bottom rail to mark a position on the partition for the hanging bar.

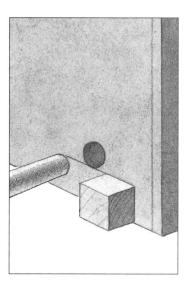

BUILT-IN PLATE RACK AND DRIP TRAY

This is a simply designed storage unit which is intended to be built-in between two wall-mounted shelf units (see opposite page for instructions and page 32 for a photograph of the unit in position). For a perfect result, great accuracy and attention to detail, as well as a pair of helping hands, is called for, but the finished unit is solid, secure, and stylish. Wooden dowels are inserted at regular intervals into three wooden rails which are angled to suit the size of your dishes. Instructions for a drip tray made from plastic laminate particleboard are also included. The drip tray allows you to leave dishes stacked on the plate rack to air dry, and save you valuable time.

TOOLS

UTILITY KNIFE

STEEL MEASURING TAPE

TRY SQUARE

BACK SAW

HAMMER

MORTISE GAUGE

POWER DRILL

DRILL BITS

COMPASS SAW $1\frac{1}{2}$–2in (38–50mm) to suit frame diameter (or use a router)

POWER SABER SAW

MALLET

ADDITIONAL TOOLS

V-BLOCK

DRILL STAND (or home-made drill guide) for accurate drilling

MATERIALS

PLATE RACK

Part	Quantity	Material	Length
FRAME	3	$1\frac{1}{2}$–2in (38–50mm) diameter softwood dowel	As required
RACK SPACERS	As required	$\frac{1}{2}$in (12mm) diameter softwood dowel	$5\frac{1}{2}$in (137mm)
RACK SPACERS	As required	$\frac{1}{2}$in (12mm) diameter softwood dowel	10in (250mm)

DRIP TRAY

Part	Quantity	Material	Length
TRAY BASE	1	$\frac{5}{8}$in (15mm) plastic laminate particleboard	As required
EDGE FRAME	4	$\frac{1}{2} \times 1\frac{1}{2}$in (12 × 38mm) hardwood edge-banding	As required
SUPPORT BATTENS	2	$\frac{3}{8} \times \frac{1}{4}$in (10 × 6mm) S4S softwood	As required

BUILT-IN PLATE RACK AND DRIP TRAY

Cut the three large frame dowels to length. To calculate the length of each dowel, measure the distance between the partitions and add 4in (100mm). The 4in (100mm) allows for 1in (25mm) either end to slot into the partitions, and 1in (25mm) excess either end. A nail can be driven into this excess to secure the dowel to the V-block while the holes are being drilled in it (*see* **Techniques, Making a V-block, page 83**). The excess will be sawn off later.

Position one dowel in the V-block. Draw a straight line along its length using a steel straight-edge resting against one side of the block (fig 1). Starting $2\frac{1}{2}$in (62mm) in from one end, mark off $1\frac{3}{8}$in (35mm) centers along it. Use a pencil or mortise gauge to do this.

Using the first dowel as a guide, transfer the $1\frac{3}{8}$in (35mm) centers to a second dowel. For the third dowel, mark a line down its length as described above, and continue the line across the end section to the center. Draw a second line, 96° to the first. Continue the second line along the length of the dowel.

Use the first dowel to transfer the $1\frac{3}{8}$in (35mm) centers to the third dowel, making the marks between the two lines. Put the first dowel in the V-block with the marked hole-centers vertical. Nail it down at either end to secure it.

DRILLING THE HOLES

Start to drill the vertical holes (*see* **Techniques, page 83**).

Each hole should be drilled to a depth of $\frac{1}{2}$in (12mm). Use a drill stand, a drill guide set at 90°, or make your own drill guide.

MAKING A DRILL GUIDE

You will need a block of 2 × 4in (50 × 100mm) lumber. Make a v-shaped cut-out in it so that it will fit neatly over the dowel resting in the V-block. Drill a hole through it vertically (see above).

Thread the drill bit through the hole in the drill guide and place the tip of the bit on the first hole. Pull the guide into position, resting on the V-block, then drill a $\frac{1}{2}$in (12mm) deep hole. Drill all of the holes required in the same way.

ASSEMBLY

Cut 1in (25mm) from each end of each of the three frame dowels. (This is the excess used when nailing the dowel to the V-block.)

By tapping gently with a mallet, fit all the $5\frac{1}{2}$in- (140mm-) long dowels into one of the frame dowels (one with a single row of holes) and all the 10in- (250mm-) long dowels into the other frame dowel.

Join the two sections together to complete the assembly. You will need help when aligning the dowels. If the fit is very tight, it will be easier to join the frame if you clamp it together in a woodworker's vise. For an extra-tight fit, clamp the rack in a vise. If the fit is loose, put a little waterproof glue in the holes to fill any gaps.

Look down the length of the rack to check if it is perfectly aligned. If it is not, twist the rack into alignment by getting one person at each end of the rack to adjust it.

SECURING THE RACK

It is essential that the plate rack is in position before the supporting partitions on either side of the rack are finally secured in place.

Lift up the rack to one of the partition sides. Tilt it back until an angle is found in which the plates will sit comfortably. Mark the dowel positions on the partition sides.

Position the wall batten in its correct place at the back of the partition so that this can be drilled at the same time.

Cut out the holes to a depth of 1in (25mm) with a power drill and a spade bit or with a router or with a compass saw.

Fit one partition in place and carefully slot the rack into it. Meanwhile, ask someone to hold the partition against the other end of the rack for you so that the position for the three holes can be marked, and the holes drilled. The partition can then be tapped into the rack to secure it in position. Finally, attach the second partition to the wall batten. You will find further ideas and instructions for a variety of wall-mounted plate racks and shelves, hanging bars, and suspended shelves on pages 68, 114, and 116.

❶ Marking Plate Rack Dowel Hole Centers
Rest dowel in a V-block and mark off centers at $1\frac{3}{8}$in (35mm) intervals. Transfer all the marks on to the second dowel. On the third dowel draw a second line at exactly 96° to the first.

❷ Using a Drill Guide
With dowel nailed into a V-block, line up on first hole. Use scrap wood as a drill guide.

❸ Drilling the Dowel Holes
A drill guide, which you can make yourself, helps to keep the drill bit vertical. Drill $\frac{1}{2}$in (12mm) holes.

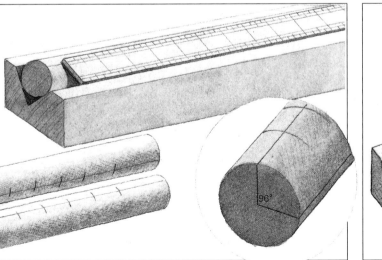

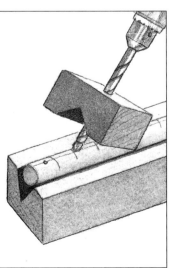

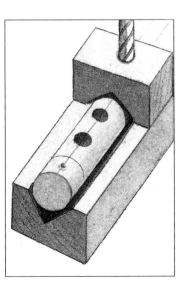

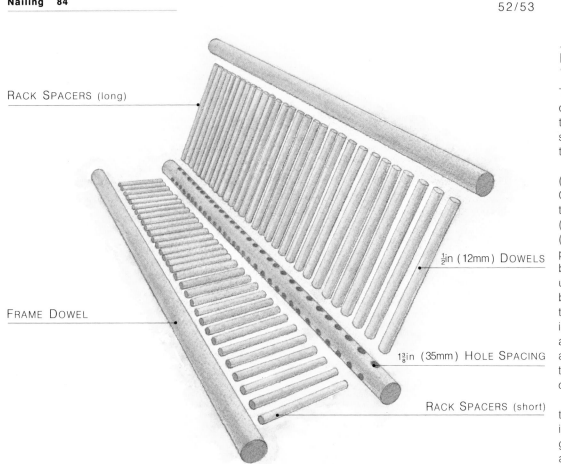

RACK SPACERS (long)

FRAME DOWEL

½in (12mm) DOWELS

1⅜in (35mm) HOLE SPACING

RACK SPACERS (short)

DRIP TRAY

This is removable for easy drying or cleaning. Cut the tray-support battens to the same length as the shelf-support battens, and nail and glue them to the bottom of the partitions.

Make a tray base from ⅝in (15mm) laminated particleboard. Cut two pieces of edge-banding to the depth of the tray. Saw ⅜in (10mm) from each to leave them 1in (25mm) high. Glue and nail the pieces of edge-banding to the tray base ends so they are flush with the underside (fig 5). Cut the front and back edge-bandings to the length of the tray plus the end edge-bandings. Nail and glue in place, leaving a ⅜in (10mm) underhang at front and back. Make small cut-outs at the back to allow the tray to slide over its support battens.

Waterproof the interior edges of the tray with a silicone bath caulking. When using a mastic applicator gun, it is easier to push the trigger away from you to provide an even flow of caulking.

❹ Positioning the Plate Rack Between Partitions
The assembled plate rack is fitted between two wall-mounted shelf partition units and slips neatly into three holes that are drilled into each partition side panel for a secure attachment.

❺ Making the Drip Tray
The plastic laminate particleboard tray, with hardboard edge-banding, rests on two support battens. End edge-banding is fixed first (*top*), then front and back edge-banding.

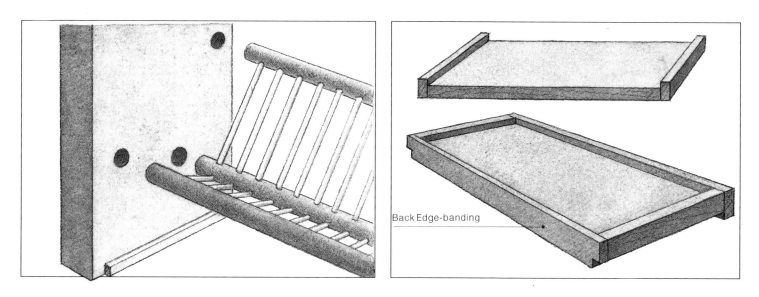

Back Edge-banding

Wall-mounted Slatted Shelves

Tools

- STEEL MEASURING TAPE
- STEEL BENCH RULE
- UTILITY KNIFE
- TRY SQUARE
- BACK SAW
- MITER BOX
- SCREWDRIVER
- DRILL (hand or power)
- COUNTERSINK DRILL BIT
- MASONRY DRILL BIT
- SPADE DRILL BIT
- SPACING BATTEN (made from an offcut of wood)

Cut a 45° miter at each end of the $1\frac{1}{2}$in (38mm) diagonal. Glue and screw together the two 1 × 3in (25 × 75mm) pieces. Use two 1in (25mm) No 8 screws.

Lay the L-shaped piece on the workbench and place the diagonal in position. Mark the diagonal's internal shoulder on the L-shape at both ends (fig 1). Continue the lines around the edges on to the backs.

Mark the position for each screw hole, $\frac{3}{4}$in (19mm) from the pencil line and centrally on the wood. Drill and countersink pilot holes. Lay the L-shaped section on the bench and place a $\frac{1}{2}$in (12mm) thick packing piece in position (fig 2). This is so that the diagonal lies centrally in the 1 × 3in (25 × 75mm) L-bracket. The diagonal can now be repositioned, and glued and screwed in place.

Make up extra brackets as required. Allow one bracket for each 48in (1200mm) of shelf span. If the shelves are likely to be heavily laden, fix the brackets every 36in (900mm).

Attaching Brackets to a Wall

The leg of the bracket that is overlapped by the other piece at the top is the one that is fixed to the wall (fig 3). Drill countersunk pilot holes and fix the brackets to the wall by means of a temporary batten, to ensure that they are level.

Materials

Part	Quantity	Material	Length
L-SHAPE BRACKETS	2	1 × 3in (25 × 75mm) S4S lumber	14in (350mm)
DIAGONAL BRACKET	1	2 × 2in (50 × 50mm) S4S lumber	$16\frac{1}{2}$in (410mm)
SLATS	5	1 × 2in (25 × 50mm) S4S lumber	As required

Optional: hanging bar of $\frac{3}{4}$in (19mm) wood dowel or metal rod

Hanging Bar

Drill holes for the bar in the brackets before securing them to the wall. Decide the distance between the brackets and cut the bar to this length plus $1\frac{1}{2}$in (38mm).

Mark on the diagonals the positions for the bar holes according to the size of the objects you intend to hang from it. Drill the holes to the same diameter as the bar and $\frac{3}{4}$in (19mm) deep. Fit the first bracket to the wall, slot in the bar, then fit the second bracket on the other end and secure it to the wall.

Fitting the Slats

Cut the slats to the required length, allowing an overlap of 3in (75mm) at each end. Fit the front slat flush with the front of the brackets. Use a single $\frac{1}{2}$in (12mm) No 6 screw in each bracket. With the back edge of the back slat butted against the wall, space the remaining slats at equal centers for a neat finish.

① Marking Brackets for Positioning the Diagonals
Screw the flat pieces of lumber together at right angles. Temporarily fit the diagonal strut. Mark off the internal shoulders and continue the lines on to the back faces of the brackets.

② Attaching Diagonal Strut
Use a suitable offcut of wood to give support to the diagonal strut when securing it in place.

③ Finished Shelf Brackets
The top rail fits on to the wall rail and the brackets are braced by the diagonal strut.

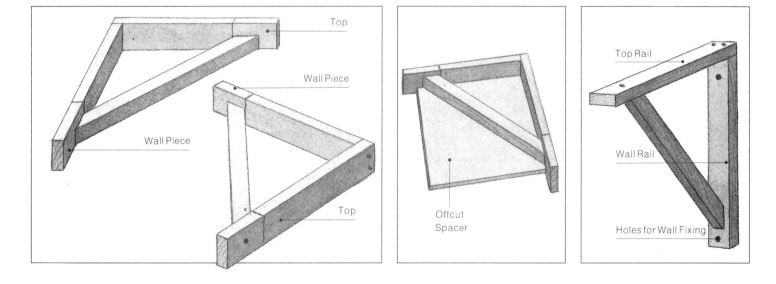

Top · Wall Piece · Wall Piece · Top · Offcut Spacer · Top Rail · Wall Rail · Holes for Wall Fixing

REMOVABLE TOWEL RAIL

Made from $1\frac{1}{2}$–2in (38–50mm) diameter dowel, available from lumberyards.

TOOLS

STEEL MEASURING TAPE

TRY SQUARE

BACK SAW

DRILL (hand or power)

DRILL BITS

HACKSAW

SCREWDRIVER

METAL FILE or EMERY CLOTH

PARING CHISEL or ROUTER

Measure the distance between the base partitions. Cut the dowel to this length. Mark 1in (25mm) in from each end and cut off a disk from each end. Mark center of each disk and the long dowel at either end.

Drill a pilot hole in one end of the dowel, then insert a $1\frac{1}{2}$in (38mm) No 8 woodscrew, leaving just the shank protruding by $\frac{1}{2}$in (12mm). Repeat at other end. Use a hacksaw to cut off the screw heads. File off any burr from the shank ends so about $\frac{5}{16}$–$\frac{3}{8}$in (8–10mm) of shank protrudes.

For the disks, drill a series of $\frac{1}{8}$in (4mm) diameter holes from the center of each disk to the edge to form a slot. The holes should be drilled to the same depth as the protruding screw shanks. To ensure this, stick tape to the drill bit at the correct distance from the tip. Use a chisel to clean out the slot. A much easier method of forming a slot is to use a router with a $\frac{1}{8}$in (4mm) diameter cutter if you have one.

Drill $\frac{1}{8}$in (4mm) diameter screw holes through each disk on either side of the center line. Hold the dowel horizontally in place and mark off the positions of the disks. Then hold each disk in position to mark off screw positions. The holes should be about 3in (75mm) below the worksurface and set back about 2in (50mm) from the front. Screw to partition and slot rail in place.

④ Fixing Brackets to the Wall and Adding the Slats
Drill holes for hanging bar and slot it in place before fitting the second bracket to the wall. Nail a batten to the wall temporarily to keep the brackets level. Screw down slats.

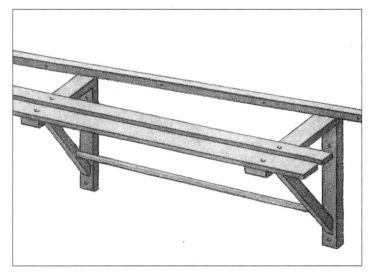

⑤ Cutting and Shaping Ends
Use a screwshank to form the rail pivot. For the slot, drill a series of holes in an offcut.

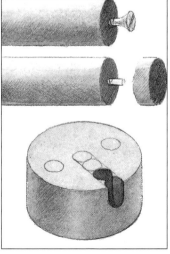

⑥ Fitting the Rail in Place
Use a narrow chisel to form a slot in the disk for the rail pivot. Screw the disks to the partition sides.

Knife Rack

Tools

STEEL MEASURING TAPE

TRY SQUARE

HAMMER

BACK SAW

TWO C-CLAMPS

DRILL (hand or power)

COUNTERSINK DRILL BIT

MASONRY DRILL BIT

SANDING BLOCK and
SANDING PAPER

A knife rack is a useful and versatile addition to the kitchen system, and this is a simple project to build.

Working from the back, glue and nail both verticals on to the first slat. Allow each end of the slat to protrude 3in (75mm) beyond the verticals (fig 1).

Fit the remaining slats at $1\frac{1}{2}$in (38mm) centers. Use a spacing batten (*see* **Techniques, page 80**) to ensure accurate spacing between the slats. Leave a space for the knife slot. Glue the $\frac{1}{4} \times 1$in (6 × 25mm) spacers to the spare slat. There should be a spacer at each end and one in the middle of the slat (fig 2).

Glue the facing piece of the knife slot over the spacers. Secure with C-clamps, allow the glue to set and then sand it down.

Fit the knife-slot section to the verticals in the center of the space remaining, working from the back.

Drill countersunk holes through the front of the rails into the wall at the desired spot. As the load is light, it is not necessary to fix the rack to the studs in a lath-and-plaster wall or a hollow wall.

Materials

Part	Quantity	Material	Length
SLATS	7	$\frac{3}{4} \times 1$in (19 × 25mm) softwood	34in (850mm)
BACK OF KNIFE SLOT	1	1 × 1in (25 × 25mm) softwood	As above
FRONT OF KNIFE SLOT	1	$\frac{1}{4} \times 1$in (6 × 25mm) softwood	As above
SPACERS	3	$\frac{1}{4} \times 1$in (6 × 25mm) softwood	2in (50mm)
VERTICALS	2	$\frac{3}{4} \times 1$in (19 × 25mm) softwood	18in (450mm)

1 **Nailing the Verticals to the Horizontal Slats**
Work from the back and nail the vertical rails to the horizontal slats leaving a space for the knife slot to be fitted. Use a spacing batten to ensure that slats are evenly spaced.

2 **Forming the Knife Slot from Lumber Battens**
The knife slot batten is thicker than the others to accommodate knife handles. The slot is formed from a thin slat laid over three offcuts which act as spacers for the knives.

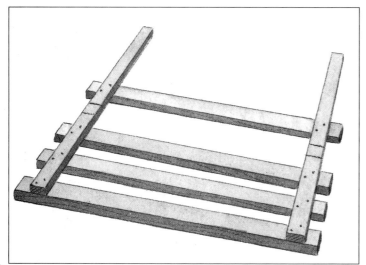

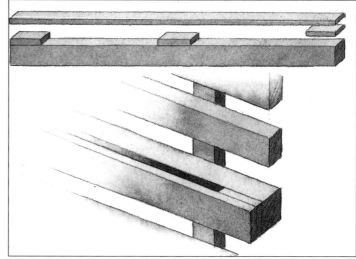

DRYING RACK

TOOLS

STEEL MEASURING TAPE

STEEL BENCH RULE

TRY SQUARE

SANDING BLOCK, COARSE and FINE SANDING PAPER

SABER SAW or HAND SAW

POWER DRILL

SPADE DRILL BIT

UTILITY KNIFE

Cut the square piece of wood in half diagonally. Round off all the corners with coarse, then fine sandpaper. Paint the wood if required.

Mark the centers for the holes in one end piece. Mark the holes at 4in (100mm) centers and 1¾in (45mm) in from the edge. Drill the six (dowel) holes to 1in (25mm) diameter and the small (rope) holes to ¼in (6mm) diameter. Clamp both end pieces together, then use the first piece as a template to mark the hole positions on the second piece. Drill the holes in the second piece. Locate the dowels in the two end pieces, leaving about 3in (75mm) protruding at either end.

Find the positions of the ceiling joists. If they run at right angles to the rack, then, after fitting the pulleys, adjust the position of each end piece to align with the pulley above it. If the ceiling joists run parallel with the rack, choose the most convenient one to fit the pulleys to. Align the end pieces with the pulleys. Fit the double pulley at the side from which you want to operate the rack.

Screw the cleat to a convenient place on the wall. Tie the rope to the rope hole in the end piece. Feed the rope through the single pulley, across to the double pulley, down to the cleat, up through the double pulley again, and then down to the other triangle. Tie this end in place to form a loop. Take up the slack rope and wind it around the cleat.

Check the rack lowers and raises correctly, then dab aliphatic resin into dowel holes to secure them.

MATERIALS

Part	Quantity	Material	Length
ENDS	1	1in (25mm) plywood (or MDF)	16in sq (400mm sq)
RAILS	6	1in (25mm) diameter hardwood dowel	6ft 6in (2m)

ONE SINGLE PULLEY, ONE DOUBLE PULLEY (screw-in or screw-on type)

A HANK OF SASH CORD, AND ONE CLEAT

---

③ Marking Drying Rack End Pieces for Rails
Two triangular end pieces are cut from a 16in (400mm) square of 1in (25mm) plywood. Mark holes at 4in (100mm) intervals on a line 1¾in (45mm) in from the side edges.

④ Hanging the Drying Rack
A double and a single pulley should be securely fitted into ceiling joists. Fit a cleat firmly to a nearby wall and arrange cords as shown so that the drying rack can be raised and lowered easily.

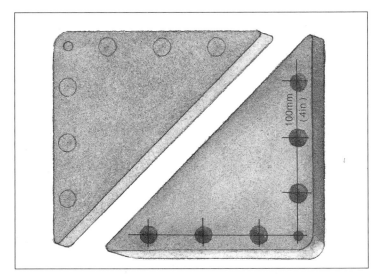

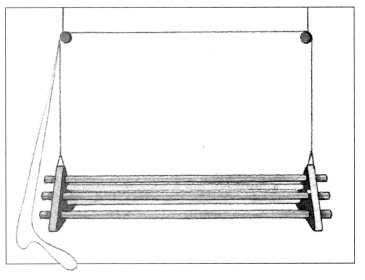

SERVING AND DISPLAY UNIT WITH MIRRORS

I built shelving similar to this a few years ago in my house in Provence, France; as it has been so successful there it seemed an ideal project for this book. It works on the principle that everybody likes to display their favorite china, bowls, platters, and pans, as these objects create an appetizing backdrop for any kitchen or dining room. The shelving is based on an idea that I first saw in a restaurant in Positano, Italy. The most important aspect of design is the panels of mirror that are slightly angled to reflect the components of the bowls and platters which sit on the shelf. In Positano wonderful bowls of antipasto were displayed and the effect was mouth-watering and demonstrated that, with a little ingenuity, less can be more. The mirror provides an entrancing double vision of a rich arrangement of food and wine, to be enjoyed while sitting at the dining table or working in the kitchen.

The design also incorporates a wide shelf that is waist high and can be used as a serving surface in a dining area. The finish you choose for the shelving unit can be varied to suit your particular decorative scheme. The wide shelf shown here is marble, which, while very effective as a display background for bowls of fruit, vegetables, and seafood, may be substituted for a more economical material if your finances are limited. But don't dispense with the mirrors!

SECTION

strip light

groove in shelf to stop plates slipping

angled mirror

marble shelf

half-round shelf

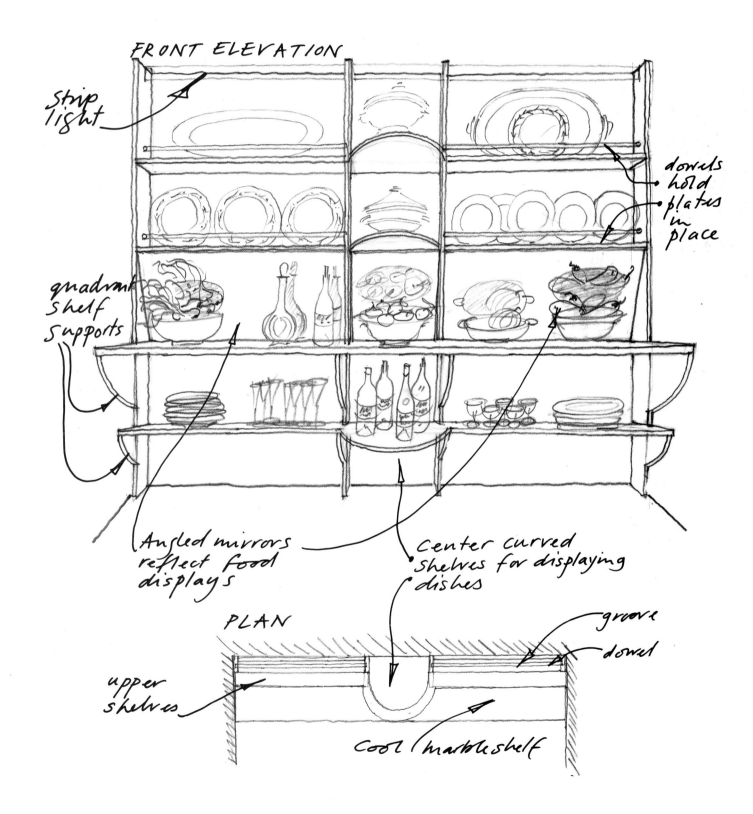

FRONT ELEVATION

strip light

dowels hold plates in place

quadrant shelf supports

Angled mirrors reflect food displays

Center curved shelves for displaying dishes

PLAN

groove

dowel

upper shelves

Cool marble shelf

SERVING AND DISPLAY UNIT WITH MIRRORS

LOWER SHELF SECTION

Using 1in (25mm) MDF, cut four verticals 30in (770mm) – the height of the underside of the serving shelf – by 6in (150mm). For the serving shelf supports, cut out four quadrants from a strip of MDF 12in (300mm) wide and at least $49\frac{1}{4}$in (1250mm) long, so that the radius of each can be 12in (300mm). Draw the shape of one quadrant before cutting it out with a Saber saw or compass saw and sanding this to a smooth curve. Use this quadrant as a pattern for marking out the remaining three quadrants. For the lower shelf supports, cut out four smaller quadrants from a strip 5in (125mm) wide by $22\frac{1}{2}$in (570mm) long, so that the radius of each can be 5in (125mm). Again, cut out one quadrant and use this as a pattern for the remainder.

FIXING QUADRANTS

Using $\frac{3}{8}$in (10mm) dowels, 2in (50mm) long, glue and attach the large quadrants to the front edges of the uprights. Use a doweling jig (or dowel points) to align the holes, ensuring that the top edges of the quadrants and uprights are flush.

Clamp each assembly and allow sufficient time for the glue to set. This will be easier if you leave square notches on the quadrants to clamp against, sawing them off later to complete the curve.

Measure 12in (300mm) up from the bottom edge of each vertical for the position of the top of the smaller quadrants. Fit all four in place as for the large quadrants.

ROUTING FOR SHELVES

The top edge of each lower quadrant aligns with and supports the bottom of each lower shelf. Use a try square and a pencil or utility knife to mark the top of the quadrant on to all of the vertical pieces where a shelf will be supported. Using a router with a $\frac{3}{4}$in (19mm) straight bit, cut out a groove to the top of the line at a depth of $\frac{1}{4}$in (6mm). Do the same on the inner faces of the end vertical pieces and then repeat the whole process on both faces of the inner vertical pieces.

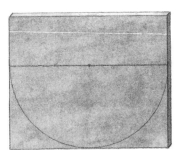

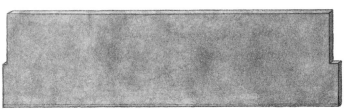

Upper Half-round Shelf
Cut from a rectangle of $\frac{3}{4}$in (19mm) MDF measuring $19\frac{1}{4} \times 15\frac{5}{8}$in (487 × 393.5mm). Measure 6in (150mm) in from the back edge and draw a line across. At center point of this line draw a semi-circle as shown.

Center Curved Shelf
Cut from a rectangle of $\frac{3}{4}$in (19mm) MDF measuring $19\frac{1}{2} \times 18$in (500 × 460mm). Mark 11in (280mm) in from the back edge. From this line draw a curve to meet front edge in center. Saw notch as shown.

Lower Straight Shelf
The span of the shelves is flexible, but they must be of equal length on each side. Shelf width is 11in (280mm). Both notches are 6in (150mm) long. The outer notch is $\frac{3}{4}$in (19mm) wide, the inner $\frac{1}{4}$in (6.5mm).

1 Assembly of Lower Vertical Partition Panel
Cut lower vertical from 1in (25mm) thick MDF. Serving shelf support is quadrant of MDF with radius of 12in (300mm). Small quadrant has 5in (125mm) radius. Fix quadrants using dowels.

2 Fitting a Lower Straight Shelf Between Partitions
Make sure that the shelves at each side are of equal length. The depth of each one should be $11\frac{1}{4}$in (280mm) including edge-banding. Shelf ends are rabbeted to cover the verticals.

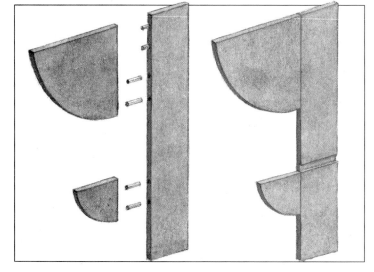

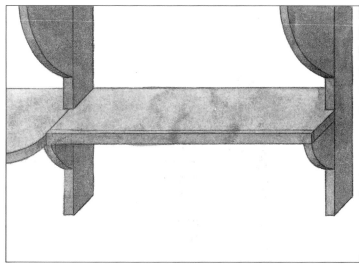

CENTER CURVED LOWER SHELF

For the center curved lower shelf, cut out a rectangle from $\frac{3}{4}$in (19mm) MDF, $18 \times 19\frac{1}{2}$in (460×500mm). The $19\frac{1}{2}$in (500mm) dimension will be the width. Mark 11in (280mm) in from, and parallel to, the back edge – this will be the depth of the straight shelf. From this line, draw and cut a curve to meet the front edge in the center. Mark 6in (150mm) in from and parallel to the back edge. Saw out notches from both sides, $\frac{1}{4}$in (6.5mm) wide and 6in (150mm) long; these locate in the grooves cut in the vertical partitions.

LOWER STRAIGHT SHELVES

Calculate how long you want your $\frac{3}{4}$in (19mm) lumber core shelves to be on each side of the curved shelf, making sure that they are of equal length. The depth of each one should be 11in (280mm) including a $\frac{1}{8}$in (3mm) edge-banding, glued and nailed to the front edge. Cut out the two shelves, then cut notches from each end – 6in (150mm) long, and $\frac{1}{4}$in (6.5mm) wide on the inner edge; $\frac{3}{4}$in (19mm) wide on the outer edge. This will ensure that they meet at the center line of the inner verticals with the curved center shelf. The outer edges of the straight shelves cross the outer verticals and finish flush with the outside of the unit.

INSTALLATION

Position one of the uprights against the wall as a guide to marking on the wall the position of the serving shelf. Mark an accurate line for the underside of the shelf along the back wall and any side wall. Using a carpenter's level, ensure that the line is level along its entire length.

Screw 1×2in (25×50mm) softwood battens along the back wall on the underside of the line to give extra support to the serving shelf. Three battens are needed, cut to fit the distance between the verti-

cal sections. If an end vertical is being attached directly into a return wall, screw directly through the upright and quadrant into the wall. Drill and generously countersink the holes – one near the top edge, one near the bottom of the vertical, and two in each quadrant. Put the upright in place and mark off the positions of the screws on the wall. Remove the vertical and drill holes for 2in (50mm) No 8 screws in the wall. Insert anchors in the holes, replace the vertical, and screw into the wall.

If the end vertical is away from a return wall then it must be secured to the back wall with $2\frac{1}{2}$in $\times 2\frac{1}{2}$in $\times \frac{5}{8}$in (65mm $\times$ 65mm $\times$ 16mm) angle brackets – one at the top and one set into the shelf notch.

The shelf notch bracket will be concealed by the shelf when this is in position. The shelf will have to be trimmed to allow for this bracket. To conceal the top bracket, attach it vertically to the wall so that the top "arm," which protrudes from the wall at a right angle, will rest in a slot cut in the top edge of the vertical partition. The back arm of the bracket should be set into a slotted groove in the wall so that it allows the rear edge of the vertical to be held firmly.

The bottom of the vertical can be secured by using a "dowel" of $\frac{1}{8}$in (3mm) diameter steel rod or bolt cut to a length of 1in (25mm) with a hacksaw. Half of the "dowel" should be sunk into the floor and the remainder into the underside of the vertical partition. The difficult part is locating the hole in the vertical partition directly over the "dowel" protruding from the floor. To do this, first secure the "dowel" in the vertical partition, then offer up the vertical in its exact position against, and at 90° to, the wall. Tap the top edge sharply with a hammer so that an impression of the "dowel" will be left in the floor. This indicates the drilling position. The "dowel" can be an easy fit since its function is simply to hold the

base of the vertical partition in place. Protect the top edge of the vertical partition with a block of scrap wood before striking it with a hammer.

Screw the protruding arm of the bracket to the top edge and secure the second bracket into the shelf rabbet and the wall.

Fit the supporting batten in place against the underside of the line, fixing it to the wall with 2in (50mm) No 8 screws at 12in (300mm) centers. Offer up the next vertical and fix it to the wall using the same method as the first. Repeat this process for the remaining two verticals, gluing in the shelves as you work along the wall. The floor "dowel" can be left out of the two middle vertical partitions.

SERVING SHELF

The serving shelf sits on the battens and verticals. If you are using marble or slate, no fixing will be necessary as its weight will be enough. For a wood shelf, use dowels to fix it to the top edges of the uprights and quadrants. If the shelf is to be painted, simply screw down into the uprights.

UPPER SHELF SECTION

Measure the distance from the top of the serving shelf to the ceiling. Measure it in three places – both ends and the middle. Take the smallest dimension, if they differ, and cut four verticals to this length from 1in (25mm) MDF. Each vertical must be 6in (150mm) wide. Measure up $25\frac{3}{4}$in (655mm) from the bottom

LIGHT

VALANCE

UPPER VERTICAL PARTITION

PLATE-RETAINING RAIL

UPPER SHELVES

HALF-ROUND SHELF

MIRROR

SERVING SHELF

CURVED CENTER SHELF

LOWER SHELF

LOWER VERTICAL PARTITION

Side Section of Display Unit
This section shows how the shelves are spaced, and the positioning of the quadrant supports of the lower shelves. Note that the mirror slopes forward to display items placed on the serving shelf.

DIVIDED SHELVES

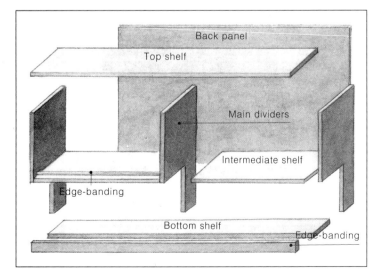

CONSTRUCTION

These kitchen shelves are ideal for storing dishes and utensils neatly and safely. The basic shelves and dividers can be made from either $\frac{3}{4}$in (19mm) laminated plywood or from $\frac{5}{8}$in (15mm) laminated particleboard. The lower shelf has a 1in (25mm) deep edge-banding on the front which is glued and nailed flush with the underside.

The upper and lower shelves run to the full width of the unit. Main vertical dividers are installed between them at 45in (1140mm) intervals and at the ends. The center shelves fit between the main dividers. If you are storing plates, glassware, and pans, you can install additional $\frac{3}{8}$in (10mm) dividing leaves between the main dividers.

Dowel joints are used for all of the components in this unit. First, the intermediate shelf units are assembled on the main upright dividers using $\frac{5}{16}$in (8mm) diameter beech dowels $1\frac{9}{16}$in (40mm) long. Then the top and bottom shelves are assem-

bled over dowels of the same size in the top and bottom edges of the main dividers.

Smaller dowels ($\frac{1}{4} \times 1\frac{1}{4}$in [6 × 30mm]) are used to attach the plywood dividers to the underside of the top shelf. The unit is covered at the back with a panel of $\frac{1}{8}$in (4mm) plywood or painted hardboard. The panel is nailed to the edges of the main dividers and shelves, and also to the thin plywood dividers.

To prevent items rolling off the intermediate shelf, you can attach either a deep edge-banding (second bay from left in the main photograph), or a hardwood beading $\frac{1}{4} \times \frac{1}{4}$in (6 × 6mm) to the shelf surface about 2in (50mm) back from the front edge (as in the bay with the dinner-plate rack).

Install the unit by screwing into the walls at each end through the end dividers, and by attaching the main dividers in the rear wall with the brackets used to hang kitchen cupboards. Whichever method is chosen, it is essential that the screws are long enough to pass through the plaster and into the masonry.

❶ The Critical Dimensions
In this exploded view, only two bays are shown, but the unit can be extended to room width. Between the main dividers, plywood dividing leaves can be installed to the undersides of the top and intermediate shelves.

❷ Jointing Main Components
Dowel joints are recommended, although dado joints can be used if greater stength is required.

❸ Mounting Plywood Dividers
These are fitted to shelf undersides using dowels or dado slots, then glued and nailed to the back panel.

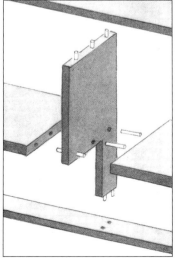

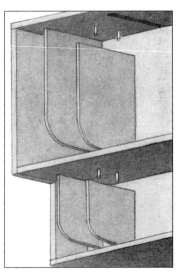

HANGING BARS

CONSTRUCTION

Hanging bars for storage make a feature of the rafters in this attic room. The rafters hold the bars a short distance from the sloping ceiling, allowing the space behind to be used for storage. A decorative dado rail above the cupboard front stops anything from slipping down.

If your attic room has a flat, sloping ceiling, then fit false rafters to the ceiling by nailing through the plaster into the real rafters beneath. Alternatively, mount the hanging bars on lumber blocks, or in wardrobe brackets. The hanging bars can be steel piping, such as black-painted electrical conduit, or the hollow tube sold for closet poles in wardrobes. This is available with a chrome, nickel, or brass finish, or with a white plastic coating. Alternatively, you can use copper piping. In all cases, a $\frac{3}{4}$in (19mm) diameter is recommended.

To support the bars, use saddle-type pipe clips screwed directly into the undersides of the rafters. Mount the lowest bars first, about 4in (100mm) above the dado rail. With a long, straight batten, pencil, and carpenter's level, mark the clip positions on the rafters. Mount the clips at each end first. Tie a string line between these to double check that they are level, then start attaching the intermediate clips, loosely at this stage, working towards the middle and using the string line as a guide. Fit the tubing into the clips, then attach the remaining screws. Use twin-thread screws (or particle-board screws) for securing the clips. Attach the second and third rails in the same way, spacing each 4in (100mm) from the rail below. If you have a flat, sloping ceiling and you intend to mount the hanging bars in wardrobe-rail support brackets, first snap a chalked string line on the surface of the ceiling to leave a horizontal line as a guide for positioning the brackets. Next, locate the rafter positions using a small metal detector (ceiling fixing nails will be driven into rafters). Attach the support brackets against the marked line using twin-threaded screws.

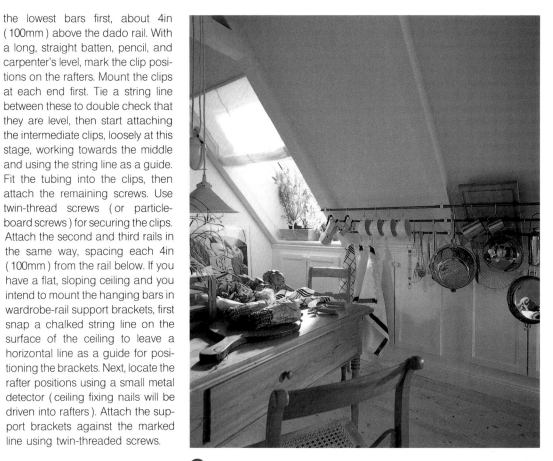

1 Attaching the Bars
Support the bars, 4in (100mm) apart, with pipe clips. Align with a carpenter's level. Saddle pipe clips (shown) look most effective, but modern equivalents are suitable. Place beveled wood anchors in the pipe ends.

2 Using Hidden Rafters
Where rafters are hidden, mount the bars in wardrobe-rail support brackets attached to the rafters. Alternatively, secure false rafters to the ceiling, or attach the hanging bars to mounting blocks, which are secured to the rafters.

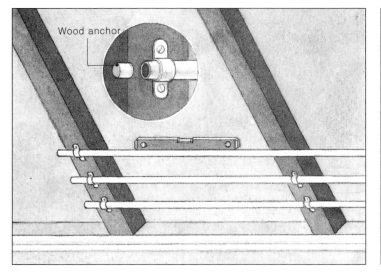

Wood anchor

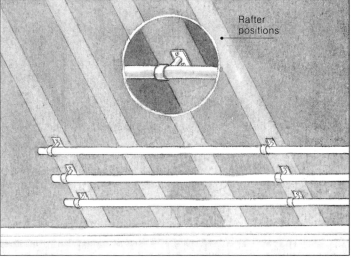

Rafter positions

SUSPENDED SHELVES

These shelves suspended over a breakfast bar make excellent use of space that would otherwise be wasted, as well as providing a light and airy divider between the kitchen and the dining area.

The shelves must be suspended securely by using steel piping secured firmly to the ceiling joists. You may be able to get chrome-steel tubing in the required lengths and threaded for attaching into screw-fixed securing plates. Metal fabricators and ships chandlers are likely sources. An alternative is to use lengths of threaded steel rods. These are covered by the steel tubing which is used for wardrobe closet poles and which is ideal for spacing the suspended shelves on the threaded rod. Closet poles are available with a chrome, nickel (matte), or brass finish, or covered with a white plastic coating.

The shelves can be solid hardwood to match the worktop, although it is perfectly acceptable to make them from a hollow lumber frame clad with plywood panels. The panels can have a hardwood ve-

neer to match the worktop. It is important that support battens are placed at regular intervals within the hollow framework.

The upper shelf can be made up and hardwood edge-banding applied around it to hide the edges of the plywood facing panels and to give the appearance of solid wood.

With the lower shelf, it is best to attach the underside facing panel *after* the shelf is in place and the nuts on the suspension rods have been tightened with a wrench.

With the hollow method of shelf building, allow for cut-outs in one edge if you wish to hang glasses by their stems. In this case, the hardwood edge-banding on that edge will have to be increased to at least the depth of the cut-outs.

To hold the shelves in their required positions, they are suspended on lengths of steel threaded rod inside steel tubes which act as spacers. Use $\frac{3}{8}$in (10mm) threaded rod which is commonly available in 36in (915mm) lengths up to 6ft (1830mm). It can be cut to length with a hacksaw, or, where the ceiling

① The Basic Construction
The shelves can be a simple lumber frame skinned with plywood sheets and edge-banded with hardwood.

② Support Batten
Lengths of threaded rod hang from a 2 × 3in (50 × 75mm) batten bolted between convenient ceiling joists.

③ Drilled Upper Shelf
Holes are drilled through cross-rails to take threaded rod. Decorative steel tubing spaces the shelves.

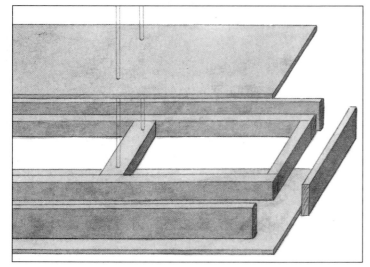

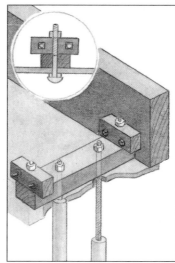

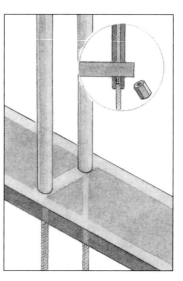

DOOR FRONTS

is high it can be extended by joining lengths with extension nuts.

At the top, the rod is bolted through holes drilled in 2 × 3in (50 × 75mm) lumber which itself is bolted (on its side) between ceiling joists above the shelving position. When making the shelf frames, work out where the hangers will be and make sure that there are frame cross-rails at these positions to give additional support.

The ¾in (19mm) steel tubing is passed over the protruding threaded rod before the upper shelf is installed and held with a nut on the rod (use an extension nut if you need to extend the rod). Shorter tubes are slipped over the threaded rod before you fit the lower shelf, which is also bolted in place on the underside. The securing nuts can be recessed into the frame cross-rails before the bottom panel is attached. With a solid wood shelf, the nuts can be fitted in pre-drilled recesses which are filled with matching anchors glued in place. The anchors are then planed and sanded flush with the surface.

❹ Concealed Nut Attachments
Drill recesses in underside of the lower shelf. If solid shelf, anchor the recesses. If hollow, fit a fascia panel.

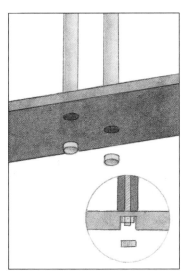

You can greatly improve the appearance of a kitchen by replacing solid cabinet doors with glazed doors. In this way the contents of the cabinets become a focal point.

It will be virtually impossible to convert the old doors, so remove them, but first noting down their dimensions, and the positions of the hinges and handles. Remove both for use on the new doors.

Make new doors from 1 × 3in (25 × 75mm) S4S lumber (the old doors were probably ¾in [19mm] thick). Cut the side rails slightly longer than required – they can be cut to the correct length later. Cut the top and bottom rails to length to allow for the type of corner joint to be used. For the strongest job, use haunched mortise and tenon joints (see **Techniques, page 89**) with the molding mitered to form a neat corner as in the diagram below. After the joints have been made and the doors assembled, the lengths of waste on the side rails can be cut off flush with the top and bottom rails. You will need a router to cut a rabbet along one edge at the back to take the glass. Turn over the frame and round over the front inner edge if required using a router fitted with a rounding over cutter.

If you do not feel confident to tackle a haunched mortise and tenon joint, you can make the door frames using dowel joints (see **Techniques, page 90**). These, if properly glued, will be strong enough.

The glass fits into the rabbet from the back of the door. It is bedded on putty and held with glass beading secured by brads. These must be driven in very carefully. Various styles of beading are available. If you do not have a router, use a molding to create a rabbet. Glue and nail it to the inner edge of the frame at the front, creating a rabbet behind for the glass to be fitted, as above. Miter the corners. Replace hinges, apply finish, and add handles.

❶ Fitting Frame and Glass
Use a haunched mortise and tenon joint (below). Rabbet frame; round front inner edge; insert glass.

❷ Alternative Method
Form rabbet by nailing molding to frame's inner edge. Secure glass with putty and beading.

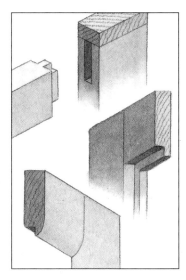

Tools

Adhesive spreader These are palm-size pieces of semi-flexible plastic with serrated or notched edges which are used to spread adhesives over wide surfaces, evenly, and at the correct rate. Because the size of the serrations or notches affects the spreading rate, adhesive manufacturers usually supply a spreader with their adhesives for brands where a spreader is required: mainly contact-types and tiling and flooring adhesives.

Bench stop and vise A woodwork vise is fitted to the underside of a bench, with the jaws level with the bench top. The jaws are lined and topped with hardwood to protect the work and any tools being used. Some vises also incorporate a small steel peg (a "dog") that can be raised above the main jaw level. This allows awkward or long pieces of wood to be clamped in position when used with a bench stop which is fixed at the opposite end of the bench stop.

Sliding bevel (1) Also called a bevel gauge, this is a type of square used to mark out lumber at any required angle. The sliding blade can be locked against the stock by means of a locking lever and the blade can form any angle with the stock.

Marking gauge (2) Essential for setting out woodworking joints, this is used to mark both widths and thicknesses with only a light scratch. The gauge comprises a handle, on which slides a stock bearing a steel marking pin. This movable stock can be locked in any position with a thumb screw so the steel pin is fixed at a precise point.

Mortise gauge (3) Similar to a marking gauge, it has two pins – one fixed, one adjustable – to mark out both sides of a mortise at the same time. Some types have an additional pin fixed below the beam so that the tool can be used as a marking gauge.

Contour gauge This is also called a shape tracer or a scribing gauge. It comprises a row of steel pins or plastic fingers held in a central bar. When pressed against an object, like a baseboard, the pins follow the shape of the object.

Utility knife A razor-sharp blade which is used to score a thin, accurate line for a saw or chisel to follow, ensuring a precise cut. The flat face of the knife can be run against the blade of a try square or straight-edge. A paring chisel is placed in the knife line for accurate paring of the last cut.

Miter box A simple open-topped wooden box which is used to guide saws into material at a fixed 45° or 90° angle, to ensure a square cut.

Plumb bob and chalk A plumb line is used to check verticals and mark accurate vertical lines, in chalk, on walls. A plumb bob is simply a pointed weight attached to a long length of string. Before use, the string can be rubbed with a stick of colored chalk. Hold the string in the required position at the top, wait for the plumb bob to stop swinging, then carefully press the string against the wall at the bottom and then pluck the string to leave a line on the wall. Most hardware stores stock chalk lines (plumb bobs with line winders and powdered chalk containers): these save time by automatically dusting the line with chalk as it is withdrawn.

Portable workbench A collapsible, portable workbench is vital for woodworking. A large, fixed workbench in a garage or shed is important, but the major advantage of the portable type is that it is lightweight and can be carried to the job, where it provides sturdy support when final adjustments have to be made.

A portable bench is like a giant vise – the worksurface comprises two sections which can be opened wide or closed tightly according to the dimensions of the work and the nature of the task. It can hold large and awkward objects.

Scribing block To fit an item neatly against a wall (which is very unlikely to be perfectly flat) the item has to be "scribed" flat to the wall using a small block of wood and a pencil (see **Techniques, page 91**). A scribing block is simply an offcut of wood measuring about 1in × 1in × 1in (25mm × 25mm × 25mm). The block is held against the wall, a sharp pencil is held against the opposite end of the block, and the block and the pencil are moved in a unit along the wall to mark a line on the item to be fitted. If you cut to this line, the item will then fit tightly against the wall.

Carpenter's level (9) Used for checking that surfaces are horizontal or vertical. A 24in (610mm) long level is the most useful all-round size. An aluminum or steel level will withstand knocks and it can be either I-girder or box-shaped in section. Ideally, a 9in (225mm) "torpedo" carpenter's level is also useful to have, for working in confined spaces such as alcoves and inside cupboards. It may be used in conjunction with a straight-edge over longer surfaces.

Steel measuring tape A 12ft (3.6m) or 18ft (5.5m) long, lockable tape (metal or plastic) is best, and one with a window in the casing that makes it easier to read measurements.

Steel bench rule Since the rule is made of steel, the graduations are very precise and indelible. A rule graduated on both sides in imperial and metric is the most useful. The rule can also serve as a precise straight-edge for marking cutting lines.

Straight-edge Can be made from a piece of 1 × 2in (25 × 50mm) scrap wood. It is used to tell whether a surface is flat and also for checking whether two points are aligned with each other.

Try square (4) An L-shaped precision tool comprising a steel blade and stock (or handle) set at a perfect right angle to each other on both

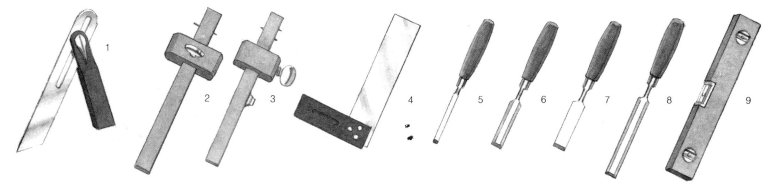

the inside and outside edges. Used for marking cutting lines at right angles to an edge and for checking a square.

SUPPLEMENTARY TOOLS

Drill stand Enables a power drill to be used with extreme accuracy when, for example, joining doweling (see **Techniques, page 90**). The hole will be perpendicular to the surface and its depth can be carefully controlled. The drill is lowered on to the work with a spring-loaded lever which gives good control and accuracy.

Metal detector Pinpoints metal objects such as electric cables and water and gas pipes hidden in walls, ceilings, and floors. Electronically operated, it buzzes or flashes when metal is found.

TOOLS FOR SHARPENING AND CUTTING

Chisels Used to cut slots in wood or to pare off thin slivers. Some chisels may be used with a mallet when cutting slots. When new, a chisel's cutting edge is ground and must be honed with an oilstone to sharpen it.

Mortise chisel (5) Used with a mallet for cutting deep slots.

Bench chisel (6) Used for undercutting in confined spaces, such as when making dovetail joints.

Firmer chisel (7) For general-purpose use around the home.

Paring chisel (8) Has a long blade for cutting deep joints or long grooves.

Doweling jig A simple doweling jig clamps on to a piece of work, ensuring that the drill is aligned accurately over the center of the dowel hole to be drilled. It also guides the drill vertically.

DRILLS

Hand drill (10) For drilling holes for screws or for making large holes, particularly in wood. It will make holes in metal and is useful where there is no power source. A handle attached to a toothed wheel is used to turn the drill in its chuck.

Power drill (11) These range from a simple, single-speed model (which will drill holes only in soft materials) to a multi-speed drill with electronic control. Most jobs call for something in between the two, such as a two-speed drill with hammer action. The two speeds enable most hard materials to be drilled and the hammer action means that you can also drill into the hardest walls.

DRILL BITS

You will need a selection of twist bits in various sizes and of different types for wood and metal, for use with a drill.

Brad-point bit (12) Used to make dowel holes in wood. The tip has two cutting spurs on the side and a center point to prevent the bit from wandering off center. Diameters range from $\frac{1}{8}$in (3mm) to $\frac{1}{2}$in (12mm).

Twist drill bit (13) Used with an electric drill for drilling small holes in wood and metal. Carbon-steel drills are for wood only: drilling into metal requires a high-speed steel drill.

Masonry bit (14) Has a specially hardened tungsten-carbide tip for drilling into masonry to the exact size required for an anchor. Special percussion drill bits are available for use with a hammer drill when boring into concrete.

Countersink bit (15) After a hole is drilled in wood, a countersink bit is used to cut a recess for the screwhead to sit in, so ensuring that it lies below the surface. Different types are available for use with a carpenter's brace and an electric drill. Head diameters are $\frac{3}{8}$in (9mm), $\frac{1}{2}$in (12mm), and $\frac{9}{16}$in (15mm). Carbon-steel bits can be used for wood, but high-speed steel bits can be used for wood, plastic, or metal.

Spade bit (16) Is used with an electric drill. It has a point at the end of the shank and its flat shank end allows it to slot into the drill chuck. Diameters are from $\frac{1}{4}$in (6mm) to 1$\frac{1}{2}$in (38mm). For maximum efficiency the bit must be turned at high speed from about 1000 to 2000 rpm. It can be used to drill into cross grain, end grain, and manmade boards. Also known as a speedbore bit.

Auger bit (17) Has a tapered, square shank that fits into a carpenter's brace. It is used to make deep holes in wood, the usual lengths being up to 10in (250mm). Diameters range from $\frac{1}{4}$in (6mm) to 1$\frac{1}{2}$in (38mm). The tip has a screw thread to draw the bit into the wood.

Forstner bit (18) A Forstner bit, or hinge-sinker bit, is primarily used for boring 1$\frac{3}{8}$in (35mm) or 1in (25mm) diameter flat bottomed holes in cabinet and wardrobe doors to accept the hinge bosses on concealed hinges. Forstner bits are used in electric drills, ideally fitted in drill stands, and set to drill no deeper than $\frac{1}{2}$in (12mm).

Oilstone and honing guide The first sharpens and the second maintains the correct angle for sharpening chisel and plane blades. An oilstone is a rectangular block of stone with grit on both sides. Oil is used as a lubricant while the blade is being sharpened on the stone, so you will need a can of fine oil nearby.

The honing guide is an inexpensive tool which makes sharpening easier and more efficient. The blade of the tool to be sharpened is inserted at an angle and clamped in place, then the guide is repeatedly rolled back and forth on the surface of the oilstone.

Power router (19) This portable electric tool is used to cut grooves, recesses, and many types of joints in lumber, as well as to shape the edges of long lumber battens to form decorative moldings. A whole range of cutting bits in different shapes and sizes is available and when fitted into the router the bits revolve at very high speed (about 25,000 rpm) to cut the wood smoothly and cleanly (20). Although hand routers (which look like small planes) are available, whenever routers are referred to in this book, it is the power router to which the remarks are directed.

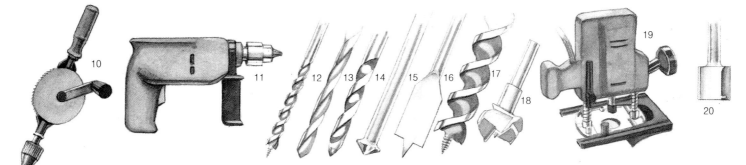

MATERIALS

LUMBER

Lumber is classified into two groups – softwoods and hardwoods. Softwoods come from evergreen trees and hardwoods from deciduous trees. Check lumber for defects before buying it. Avoid wood which is badly cracked or split, although you need not be concerned about fine, surface cracks since these can be planed, sanded, or filled. Do not buy warped wood, as it will be impossible to work with. Check for warping by looking along the length of a board to see if there is any bowing or twisting.

When you get your wood home, condition it for about ten days. As the wood will have been stored in the open air at the yard, it will be "wet." Once indoors, it dries, shrinks slightly and will warp unless stored flat on the ground. If you build with wood as soon as you get it home, your structure could run into problems later as the wood dries out. To avoid warping and aid drying, stack boards in a pile, with offcuts of wood placed between each board to allow air to circulate. This will lower the moisture content to about 10% and condition the wood, ready for use.

Softwood Softwood is much less expensive than hardwood and is used in general building work. Softwood is sold either by the *lineal* foot or the *board* foot. The former is based on the length of a piece of wood – for example, 8ft of 1 by 2 (1 × 2in [25 × 50mm]). The board foot is calculated by the thickness in inches × width in feet × length in feet – for example, 10ft of 1 by 6 would be 5 board feet: 1in × ½ft (6in) × 10ft.

It is important to remember that standard softwood sizes refer to sawn sizes – that is, how it is sawn at a mill. When bought this way, softwood is suitable only for rough constructional work such as floor joists and basic frames. However, the smooth wood used for the projects in this book, for which appearance and accuracy are important, will need to have been planed. This is the state in which softwood is commonly sold in

local lumberyards; in the trade it is referred to as "S4S" (smooth 4 sides), and, since planing takes a little off each face, planed softwood is $\frac{1}{4}$–$\frac{3}{4}$in (6–9mm) smaller in width and thickness than its stated size. Standard sizes should, therefore, be thought of as rough guides rather than exact measurements.

Hardwood Expensive and not as easy to obtain as softwoods, hardwoods often have to be ordered or bought from a specialist lumberyard. Many lumberyards will machine-plane lumber to your exact specifications. In home woodwork, hardwood is usually confined to moldings and beadings, which are used to give exposed sawn edges a neat finish.

SHEET MATERIAL BOARDS

Sheet material boards are mechanically made from wood and other fibers. They are versatile, relatively inexpensive, made to uniform quality, and are available in large sheets. Sheet materials are graded according to the quality of finished surfaces. It is worth buying the best you can afford, bearing in mind the purpose for which you will be using it. You need to know the advantages of each type of board before making your choice. All boards are made in sheets of 4 × 8ft (1220 × 2440mm), and most stockists will saw them to the size you require.

Hardboard Also called masonite, and the best known fiberboard. Common thicknesses are $\frac{1}{8}$in, $\frac{3}{16}$in, and $\frac{1}{4}$in (3mm, 4mm, and 6mm). As hardboard is weak and has to be supported on a framework, it is essentially a material for paneling. Denser types of tempered hardboard can be used for cladding partitions; softer types for bulletin boards.

Medium board Softer and weaker than hardboard, it is often, therefore, used in thicker sheets – usually $\frac{1}{2}$in (12mm).

Medium-density fiberboard (MDF) A good, highly compressed, general-purpose building board. You may find that it has to be ordered from a plywood wholesaler (your retail yard can do this for you), but it is worth it since it does not flake or splinter when cut, and leaves a clean, hard-sawn edge which does not need to be disguised as do other fiberboards. It also takes a very good paint finish, even on its edges. Thicknesses range from around $\frac{3}{16}$in to 1$\frac{3}{8}$in (5mm to 35mm).

Particleboard Made by binding wood chips together under pressure, it is rigid, dense, and fairly heavy. Particleboard is strong when reasonably well supported, but sawing it can leave an unstable edge and can also quickly blunt a saw. Ordinary screws do not hold well in particleboard, and it is best to use twin-threaded screws (*see* **Screws, page 78**). Most grades of particleboard are not moisture-resistant and will swell up when wet. Thicknesses range from $\frac{1}{4}$–1$\frac{1}{2}$in (6–40mm), but $\frac{1}{2}$in, $\frac{3}{4}$in, and 1in (12mm, 19mm, and 25mm) are the most common.

Particleboard is widely available with the faces and edges veneered with natural wood, PVC, or plastic laminates. Colored finishes and imitation wood-grain effects are also available.

If used for shelving, particleboard must be well supported on closely-spaced brackets or bearers. The better-quality laminated boards are far stronger than plain particleboard.

Plywood Made by gluing thin wood veneers together in plies (layers) with the grain in each ply running at right angles to that of its neighbors. This gives the board strength and helps prevent warping. The most common boards have three, five, or seven plies. Plywood is graded for quality, taking into the account the amount of knots and surface markings present: N is perfect but often has to be ordered, followed by A, B, C, and D in decreasing order of quality; D is for rough work only. For example, A2 means that both faces are of very good quality; AC or ACX (the "X" stands

MOLDINGS (see page 78)

Square

Rectangular

Scoop

Quarter round

Corner

for exterior) denotes A grade on one side and C on the other, and is a good, economical option where only one side will be visible.

MR (moisture-resistant) plywood is for *internal* jobs where damp conditions prevail. Plywood is available with a range of surface veneers such as teak or mahogany, or with a plastic finish. Common thicknesses are $\frac{1}{8}$in, $\frac{1}{4}$in, $\frac{1}{2}$in, and $\frac{3}{4}$in (3mm, 6mm, 12mm, and 19mm).

Lumber core Made by sandwiching natural lumber strips between wood veneers, the latter usually of Far Eastern redwood or plain birch. Although plain birch is a little more expensive than redwood, it is of a much better quality. Lumber core is very strong, but can leave an ugly edge when sawn (gaps often appear between the core strips), making edge fixings difficult. It is graded in the same way as plywood and common thicknesses are $\frac{1}{2}$in, $\frac{3}{4}$in, and 1in (12mm, 19mm, and 25mm). It is a very rigid board and is therefore ideal for a long span of shelving.

Tongued-and-grooved boards Also called match boarding, or matching, this is widely used for cladding frameworks and walls. Each board has a tongue on one side and a slot on the other side. The tongue fits into the slot on the adjacent board to form an area of cladding; this expands and contracts according to temperature and humidity without cracks opening up between boards.

Ordinary tongued-and-grooved boards fit together like floorboards, but tongued and grooved boards for cladding have some form of decoration; this can be a beaded joint, or, more commonly, beveled edge which forms the attractive V-joint of tongued, grooved, and V-jointed (TGV) boards.

ADHESIVES AND FILLERS

Adhesives Modern types are strong and efficient. If they fail, it is because the wrong adhesive is being used or the manufacturer's instructions are not followed carefully. For all general indoor woodworking, use an aliphatic resin (yellow woodworker's glue) – all glue manufacturers produce their own brands. Use a two part resorcinol glue (guaranteed waterproof) in areas where there may be water splashing or condensation. If joints do not meet perfectly, use a gap-filling adhesive.

Ceramic tiles require their own special adhesive (of a thick, buttery consistency) which is supplied, ready mixed, in tubs. If tiles are likely to be regularly splashed – around sinks for example – you should use a waterproof tile adhesive. Some brands of adhesive can also double as grouting cement for filling the gaps between tiles.

Fillers If the wood is to be painted over, use a standard plastic wood filler – the type for repairing cracks in walls. This dries white and will be evident if used under any other kind of finish. When a clear finish is needed, fill cracks and holes with a proprietary wood filler or stopping. These are thick pastes and come in a range of wood colors. You can mix them together or add a wood stain if the color you want is not available. It is best to choose a color slightly paler than the surrounding wood, since fillers tend to darken when the finish is applied. Test the filler first on a waste piece of matching wood.

In fine work, a grain-filler is used to stop the final finish sinking into the wood. This is a paste, thinned with white spirit, and then rubbed into the surface. It is supplied in a range of wood shades.

FINISHES

The choice of finish is determined by whether the wood or board will be hidden, painted, or enhanced by a protective clear finish.

LACQUER

Quick-drying cellulose lacquer is the best finishing treatment to apply to wood furniture. It is resistant to heat, scratches, and solvents, and, when sprayed on, produces a superb finish.

POLISHES

French polish Refers to a particular polish, but it is also the collective term for all polishes made with shellac and alcohol. French polish is ideal where a light to medium brown tone is required. Although it gives a fine reflection, the finish itself is not highly protective.

Button polish Will give a more golden or orange tone.

White French polish or **transparent polish** Produces a clear finish, allowing the natural color of the wood to show through. French polishing demands great skill, and many people prefer to apply a clear polyurethane varnish with a conventional wax polish covering it.

PAINT

A liquid gloss (oil-based) paint is suitable for wood, and is applied after a suitable undercoat. Generally, two thin coats of gloss are better than one thick coat. Non-drip gloss paint is an alternative. It has a jelly-like consistency and does not require an undercoat, although a quality finish may need a second coat. Use a liquid gloss if you want to spray paint.

VARNISH

Normally applied by brush, varnish can also be sprayed on. It is available as a gloss, satin, or matt finish, all clear. However, varnish also comes in a range of colors, so that you can change the color of the wood and protect it simultaneously. The color does not sink into the wood, so that if the surface becomes scratched or marked then its original color will show through. For this reason, a wood stain or dye is sometimes used to change the color of wood. It sinks into the wood, but offers no protection, so a varnish or clear lacquer will also be needed.

Half round

Twice rounded

Hockey stick

Reeded

Astragal

MOLDINGS, BATTENS, AND DOWELS

Moldings Wood moldings are used as ornamentation and to cover gaps or fixtures in a wooden construction. The term "molding" encompasses everything from a simple, thin edge-banding to architraves and baseboards. A variety of shaped cutters produce many different shapes and sizes. In the unlikely event of your being unable to buy the shape of molding you want, you could make your own using a router.

Moldings are cut from hardwood – usually poplar or basswood. You can buy more exotic hardwood moldings, mahogany for example, from a specialist lumberyard. These are expensive and you may well prefer to buy a cheaper molding and then to stain or varnish it to obtain the color that you want.

Decorative moldings are available in standard lengths of 6ft, 8ft, 10ft, and 12ft. The following types are among those which are ideal for edging manmade boards and are available in a variety of sizes: half round (or bullnose); twice rounded; hockey stick; reeded; and astragal. Square or rectangular moldings range from $\frac{1}{4} \times \frac{1}{4}$in ($6 \times 6$mm) up to $\frac{1}{4} \times 1$in (6×25mm).

Other types of molding include scoop and quarter round, which cover gaps between the meeting parts of a structure. Corner moldings are a plain version of the scoop, and can be used inside or outside a joint.

When buying moldings, check each one to make sure that the length is straight and free from large or dead knots, which are likely to fall out and leave holes. Fungal staining is something else to watch for, especially if you intend to use a clear finish. If you need several lengths of moldings for the same job, check that you get a good match. Have a close look at the edges, color, and grain of each length, since mismatching can leave surface ripples or uneven edges.

Battens A general term used to describe a narrow strip of wood. The usual sizes are 1 × 1in (25 × 25mm) or 1 × 2in (25 × 50mm).

Battens serve one of two main functions. They can be screwed to a wall to serve as bearers for shelves. Alternatively, they can be fixed in a framework on a wall, with sheet material or boards mounted over them to form a new "wall."

Dowels Used to make framework joints or to join boards edge-to-edge or edge-to-face.

Hardwood dowels are sold in diameters of $\frac{1}{4}$in, $\frac{3}{8}$in, and $\frac{1}{2}$in (6mm, 9mm, and 12mm). You can buy packs of dowels cut to length (either 1in or 1$\frac{1}{2}$in [25mm or 38mm]), or you can buy long lengths and cut them to size. Generally speaking, dowel lengths should be about one-and-a-half times the thickness of the boards being joined.

Dowels are used in conjunction with adhesive and, when the joint is complete, it is important to let excess adhesive escape from the joint. Dowels with fluted (finely grooved) sides and beveled ends will help this process. If you have plain rather than shaped dowels, make fine sawcuts along the length and bevel the ends yourself.

NAILS

Nails are generally sold by their penny (or "d") size. The most common are 2d (1in), 4d (1$\frac{1}{2}$in), 6d (2in), 8d (2$\frac{1}{2}$in), and 10d (3in).

Common nails With large, flat, circular heads, these are used for strong joints where frames will be covered, and the nails will be hidden.

Annular threaded nails Used where really strong attachments are required.

Round finishing nails Used when the finished appearance is important. The heads of these nails are driven flush with the wood's surface or countersunk so they are unobtrusive. They are also used when nailing a thin piece of wood to a thicker piece and there is a risk of splitting the wood. This is likely when nailing close to the end of the wood, or if the nail is too large.

Brads For attaching thin panels, these fine, round wire nails will be required. These have tiny, unobtrusive heads that can be driven in flush with the wood's surface or punched below it.

Hardboard pins Copper-plated and with a square cross-section. They have deep-drive diamond-shaped heads that sink into the surface – ideal for securing hardboard and other boards to lumber in areas subject to condensation, where steel pins could cause black staining.

Masonry nails For securing lumber battens to walls as an alternative to screwing and anchoring. Where a quick and permanent attachment is required, use the hardened-steel type.

SCREWS

All types of screws are available with either conventional slotted heads or with Phillips heads. The latter look neater and are the better type to use, especially if you are inserting screws with an electric screwdriver.

For most purposes, screws with flat heads are ideal as, when countersunk, the head lies flush with the surface after insertion. Round-head screws are used for attaching metal fixtures such as shelf brackets and door bolts, which have punched-out rather than countersunk screw holes. Ovalhead screws are often used alone or with metal screw cups where a neat appearance is important.

Wood screws These have a length of smooth shank just below the head. When joining two pieces of wood, this produces a strong clamping effect as the screw is tightened, but there is also a possibility of the unthreaded shank splitting the wood, so extra care is required.

Twin-threaded screws Quicker to insert than ordinary wood screws and less likely to split wood. Except for larger sizes, they are threaded along

NAILS AND SCREWS

1 Screw cup; 2 Wall anchor bolt; 3 and 4 Frame fixing (nylon plug and plated screw); 5 Veneer pin; 6 Hardboard pin; 7 Brad; 8 Round finishing nail; 9 Common nail; 10 Annular threaded nail; 11 Masonry nail; 12 Countersunk screw with slotted head; 13 Countersunk screw with Phillips head; 14 Round-head screw; 15 Ovalhead screw; 16 Dome-head screw; 17 Twin-threaded screw

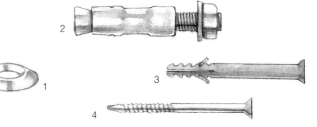

their entire length, giving an excellent grip in wood, and also in fiberboard, particleboard, lumber core, and plywood. The best types are zinc-plated (rust-resistant) and hardened (stronger and less prone to head damage by an ill-fitting screwdriver).

WALL FIXTURES AND BOLTS

The choice of wall fixture depends on the type of wall and the size and weight of the object being attached to it.

Anchors Use a masonry drill bit to drill a hole which matches the size of screw being used (a No 10 bit with a No 10 screw, for example). Insert the anchor in the hole, then insert the screw through the object being fitted and into the anchor. Tighten the screw for a secure attachment.

Solid wall fixtures The method of attaching to a solid brick or block wall is to use an anchor. Traditional fiber anchors have been superseded by plastic versions which will accept a range of screw sizes, typically from No 8 to No 12.

Stud wall fixtures To guarantee a secure fixture, you should locate the lumber uprights (studs) which form the framework of the wall and drive screws into them. If you want to attach something heavy and the lumber uprights are not in the required position, then you must attach horizontal battens to the lumber uprights, since otherwise the fitting will be unsafe.

Cavity-wall fixtures Used on hollow walls, which are constructed from wallboard partition or lath and plaster, which are found in modern and old houses respectively. There are many types of these fixtures including spring toggle, gravity toggle, and nylon toggle, and nearly all of them work on the same principle: expanding wings open up to grip the back of the wallboard or lath and plaster, securing the attachment.

Wall anchor bolt For heavier objects, such as a kitchen unit which will be heavily loaded, a more robust attachment using a wall anchor bolt is advisable. It is similar to an anchor in principle, but has its own heavy-duty machine screw. You need to make a much larger hole in the wall, typically $\frac{3}{8}$in (10mm) in diameter. The sleeve of the anchor expands in the hole as the bolt is tightened and grips the wall firmly.

LATCHES

Magnetic catches Most useful on smaller doors which are unlikely to distort. There must be perfect contact between the magnet fitted to the cabinet frame and the strike plate which is fitted to the door. The other important factor is the pulling power of the magnet – on small cabinet doors a "pull" of $4\frac{1}{2}$–$6\frac{1}{2}$lb (2–3kg) is sufficient. On wardrobe doors an 11–13lb (5–6kg) "pull" is needed.

Magnetic push latches are also useful, especially for small, lightweight doors. Push on the door inwards and it springs open just enough to be grasped and fully opened by the fingers.

Mechanical latches Common types are the spring-loaded ball catch and the roller catch. Again, alignment is vital to success, which is why adjustable types are favored. A mechanical push latch is activated by pressure on the door itself, so a door handle is not necessary.

Peglock catches Particularly suitable for kitchen and bathroom cabinets, where atmospheric conditions can cause doors to warp.

HINGES

The easiest types of hinge to fit are those which do not have to be recessed into the door or door frame – flush, decorative flush (for lightweight doors), or cranked (for cupboard doors). For fitting flaps, piano hinges are used. They are sold in 6ft (1.8m) lengths, and are cut to the required size with a hacksaw. For fitting heavy doors or for

a very neat finish, butt hinges, which are recessed, are a good alternative.

Concealed (or European) hinges are used for particleboard and MDF doors. A special drill bit is required to cut cylindrical holes in the door, but the hinges are adjustable once fitted.

SLIDING DOOR TRACKS

Doors can either be suspended from above or supported from below. The track for glass or panel doors is made from PVC and comes in a variety of colors. The door simply slides along the channel in the track.

Top-hung track Small tongued sliders or adjustable wheel hangers attached to the top edge of the door sit in the track. Small guides keep the bottom edges of the door aligned.

Bottom-roller track The door slides on small rollers located in the track. Guides attached at the top of the door keep it aligned in the track.

TILES

Ceramic tiles Especially popular for kitchens and bathrooms, where durable and waterproof surfaces are essential. There is an enormous range available, and prices vary according to size, shape, and the purpose for which they are required: floor tiles need to be much stronger than wall tiles. Common sizes are $4\frac{1}{4} \times 4\frac{1}{4}$in (108 × 108mm) and 6 × 6in (150 × 150mm), but rectangular shapes are also widely available.

"Universal" tiles have angled edges which ensure that uniform joint spacing is left when the tiles are butted up against each other.

Tiles are sold by the square foot or in boxes of 25 or 50, which will cover one half or one square yard (meter). After calculating the number of tiles required, allow a few extra to cover breakages. Unless you are using only one box, do not use the tiles straight from the box – mix them up with other boxes to disguise any slight color variations.

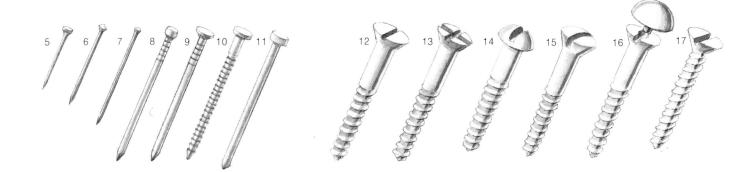

5 6 7 8 9 10 11 12 13 14 15 16 17

Wood

Wood is available either sawn or planed. Sawn wood is rough in appearance, but is close in width and thickness to the dimensions you specify when ordering. Planed wood is smoothed on all sides, but planing removes $\frac{1}{4}-\frac{3}{4}$in (6–19mm) from both the nominal width and the thickness. Sawn wood is ideal for building frameworks, but choose planed wood where a smooth finish is important. Wood should be straight and relatively knot-free. The surface should also be undamaged.

When building a framework of critical thickness (such as the basic kitchen unit modules on page 40) you may find it difficult to obtain wood of exactly the required thickness. If so, buy wood that is slightly oversized and plane it down.

After building, a fine surface can be obtained by sanding, either by hand with sanding paper wrapped around a sanding block, or by using an electric orbital sander. In both cases, start with medium-grade sanding paper and finish with fine, and only sand in line with the grain, rather than across it, as this can scratch the wood.

Wood finishes If a varnish, wax polish, or paint finish is required, it can be applied easily with a brush (or rag). An alternative, often used by professional furniture makers, is to finish woodwork with a quick-drying cellulose lacquer (*see* **Materials, page 77**), which can be applied with a paint sprayer. Before spraying, make sure that any holes are filled with stainable wood filler, and stain the surface, if required, before sanding it smooth. The first coat of lacquer is applied as a sealer. Leave it to dry for 30–60 minutes, then rub down the surface with fine sanding paper. Next, apply a second, finishing, coat of lacquer.

Measuring and Marking Square

Mark cutting lines lightly with a hard pencil, then use a utility knife to score against a straight-edge or try square along the rule to create a sharp, splinter-free line.

To mark lumber square, use a try square with the stock (handle) pressed against a flat side of the lumber, called the face side or face edge. Mark a line along the square, using a knife in preference to a pencil, then use the square to mark lines down the edges from the face mark. Finally square the other face side, checking that the lines join up right around the lumber.

Check a try square for accuracy by pressing it against a straight-edge. Mark along the blade, then turn the handle over to see if it aligns with the line from the other side.

If you are measuring and marking a number of pieces of the same length, then clamp them together and mark across several of them at the same time.

Spacing Batten

This is simply an offcut of wood, about $\frac{3}{4}$in or 1in square (19mm or 25mm square), which is used to ensure that any slats to be fixed across a frame are spaced an equal distance apart. To ascertain the length to cut the spacing batten, simply bunch all the slats at one end of the frame. Measure to the other end of the frame and divide by the number of spaces (which you can count while you have the slats laid side by side). The resulting measure is the length to cut the spacing batten, which is used to set each slat into its exact position.

Bracing

When making a door or any similar frame, it is vital that it should be square, with corners at perfect right angles. You can ensure this by using one of two bracing methods.

3-4-5 method Measure three units along one rail, four units down the adjacent rail, then nail a bracing batten accurately to one of the unit marks. Pull into square so that the bracing batten measures five units at the other unit mark, forming the long side of a triangle. Saw off the batten ends flush with the frame but do not remove the batten until frame is fitted in place. For large doors such as those on wardrobes, fix two battens on opposing corners.

---

① Marking Lumber to Length and Square All Around
Mark across the face of the lumber with a utility knife held against a try square blade. Move knife around corners and mark sides, and finally mark other side to join up the lines.

② Using Spacing Battens to Space Out Slats Evenly
Bunch the slats together evenly at one end of the frame, then measure to the other end of the frame. Divide this number by the number of spaces required; cut spacing batten(s) to this length.

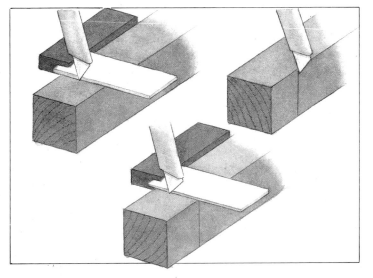

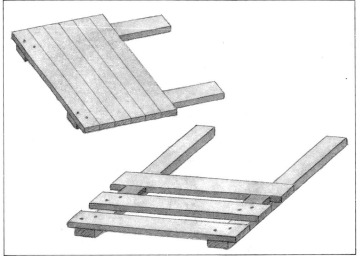

Try square method Nail a batten into one rail, pull into square by using a try square, and then nail the batten into the adjacent rail.

MAKING FOLDING WEDGES

Folding wedges are very useful for clamping large frames on a bench top during assembly. Folding wedges are always used in pairs, but more than one pair may be used to hold a large framework.

Make each pair of wedges from a piece of lumber (hardwood is ideal for this) measuring $1\frac{1}{2}$in × $1\frac{1}{2}$in × 13in (38mm × 38mm × 330mm). Make the wedges by sawing the lumber diagonally into two pieces.

To use the wedges, a wooden batten is first nailed to the bench and the item to be clamped is placed against the batten. Another batten is nailed to the bench, parallel with the first, and about $1\frac{3}{4}$in (45mm) away from the item. The wedges are now placed between the item and the second batten. The ends of the wedges are then knocked inwards with two hammers, thereby clamping the frame.

③ **Bracing a Frame Square**
Nail a batten across a corner of the frame so that the 3-4-5 shape triangle is formed.

SAWING AND CUTTING

Cross-cutting to length by hand Hold the lumber firmly with the cutting line *(see* **Measuring and Marking Square, page 80** *)* overhanging the right-hand side of the workbench (if you are right-handed). With the saw blade vertical and the teeth on the waste side of the line, draw the handle back to start the cut. To prevent the saw from jumping out of place, hold the thumb joint of your other hand against the side of the saw blade.

Rip-cutting by hand With the lumber or board supported at about knee height, start the cut as described above, then saw down the waste side of the line, exerting pressure on the down cut only. If the saw blade wanders from the line, clamp the edge of a lumber batten exactly above the cutting line on the side to be retained, and saw along it.

Using a portable power saw If the cutting line is only a short distance from a straight edge, adjust

④ **Making Folding Wedges**
Saw wood diagonally. Nail batten to bench; wedges fit between batten and item being clamped.

the saw's fence so that when it is run along the edge of the lumber, the blade will cut on the waste side of the cutting line. If the lumber is wide, or the edge is not straight, clamp a batten to the surface so that the saw blade will cut on the waste side of the line when it is run along the batten.

Ensuring a straight cut When cutting panels or boards using a power circular saw or a Saber saw, the best way to ensure a straight cut is to clamp a guide batten to the surface of the work, parallel with the cutting line, so that the edge of the base plate can be run along the batten. Obviously, the batten position is carefully adjusted so that the blade cuts on the waste side of the cutting line. Depending on which side of the cutting line the batten is clamped, when using a circular saw, it is possible the motor housing will damage the batten or the C-clamps holding it in place. In this case, replace the batten with a wide strip of straight-edged plywood clamped to the work far enough back for the motor to clear the clamps.

⑤ **Cross-cutting to Length**
Hold the lumber firmly. Steady the saw blade with your thumb joint as you start to cut.

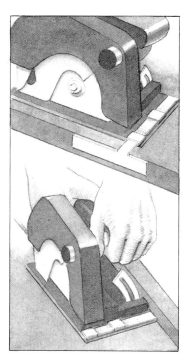

⑥ **Straight Power-saw Cutting**
Top Use the rip fence of the saw if cutting near the edge. *Above* Cutting alongside the batten.

⑦ **Cutting with a Back Saw**
Start the cut as for a hand saw. As the cut progresses keep the blade horizontal.

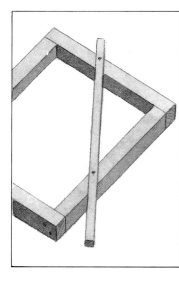

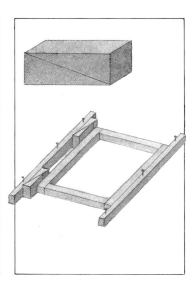

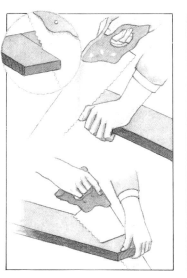

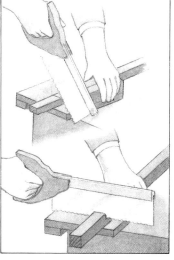

TECHNIQUES: CUTTING AND PLANING

CUTTING A CIRCLE

With a Saber saw Mark the circle on the face of the panel. If you do not have a compass, a good makeshift alternative can be made with a loop of string pivoting on a thumb tack at the circle's center. Hold a pencil vertically in the loop at the perimeter to draw the circle.

For a neat, splinter-free edge, carefully score around the cutting line with a sharp utility knife.

To start the cut, drill a hole about ⅜in (10mm) in diameter just on the waste side of the line. Insert the Saber saw blade through this hole and start the cut from this point, sawing carefully just on the waste side of the cutting line. By scoring the cutting line it will be easier to follow the line and get a smooth edge.

With a coping saw Mark out the circle, score the cutting line, and drill a hole just on the waste side as above. Disconnect the blade from one end of the frame, pass the blade through the hole, and re-connect it to the frame. It will be best to clamp

the piece of work vertically when cutting the circle. The blade can be turned in the frame as necessary to help the frame clear the piece of work, but even so, with a coping saw you will be restricted in exactly how far you are able to reach away from the piece of work. If the circle is some way from the edge, use either a power Saber saw or a hand compass saw to cut it.

With a compass saw A compass saw, similar to a keyhole saw, has a stiff, triangular pointed saw blade attached to a simple handle. A very useful compass saw blade is available for fitting in a knife handle.

Because this saw has no frame, it is very useful for cutting circles and other apertures, like keyholes, anywhere in a panel.

Preparation of the circle for cutting, such as marking out, scoring, and drilling for the blade, is the same as for the other methods. When cutting with a compass saw, keep the blade vertical and make a series of rapid, short strokes without exerting too much pressure.

CUTTING CURVES

The technique is basically the same as for cutting a circle, except that there will be no need to drill a hole in order to start the cut. You can use a Saber saw, coping saw, or compass saw to make the cut. A coping saw is ideal for making this cut because most of the waste can be removed with an ordinary hand saw, since you will be cutting close to the edge of the wood, and the saw frame, therefore, will not get in the way.

CUTTING GROOVES AND SLOTS

The easiest way to cut grooves (or dados) is to use a router with a bit set to the depth required for the groove. Use a straight-sided router bit. Ideally, the router bit should be the exact width of the groove or slot, so that it can be cut from one setting. If this is not possible, then use a smaller router bit and cut the groove or slot in two or more goes. Make the first cut along the waste side of the line with a batten clamped in line with the

groove to guide the base of the router. If a deep groove is required, it may be necessary to make a shallow cut first, then a deeper one.

To cut dados by hand, start by marking out the groove with a utility knife which will ensure a neat finish. Hold the piece of work on a bench, and with a back saw, make vertical cuts just inside the marked lines to the depth of the dado. If the dado is wide, make a series of other vertical cuts in the waste wood. Now chisel out the waste, working from each side to the middle. Finally, with the flat side of the chisel downwards, pare the bottom of the dado so that it is perfectly flat.

CUTTING RABBETS

A rabbet is an L-shaped step in the edge of a piece of lumber.

To cut a rabbet by hand, use a marking gauge to mark the rabbet width across the top face of the piece of work and down both sides. Mark the depth of the rabbet across the end and sides.

Hold the lumber flat and saw down on the waste side of the marked line

---

① Straight Rip-cutting
Clamp a straight batten alongside the cutting line and saw beside the batten. A wedge holds the cut open.

② Using a Power Saber Saw
For a straight cut, clamp a batten alongside line. Cut a circle by following line.

③ Cutting Circles by Hand
1 Drill a small hole and cut circle using a compass saw. 2 Making the cut with a coping saw.

④ Chiseling a Groove
After making saw cuts at side, chisel out waste from each side. Finally pare base flat.

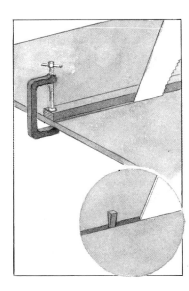
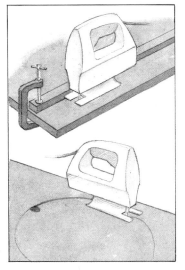
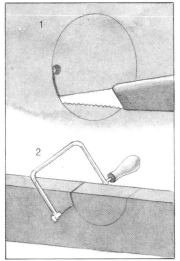

to the depth of the rabbet. Then use a chisel to cut out the waste one bit at a time along the end grain.

It is very easy to cut a rabbet using a router, and in this case it is not necessary to mark out the rabbet unless you want a guide to work to. However, do practice on scrap wood to be sure of setting the router to cut to the correct depth and width.

If using a straight cutter, adjust the guide fence on the router so that the cutter cuts to the correct width, then adjust the cutting depth so that the router will cut to the correct depth. When the router is correctly set up, simply hold it flat on the piece of work and move it against the direction of the cutter's rotation.

If you are using a cutter with a guide pin, simply adjust the depth of cut and then run the cutter along the edge of the wood to form the rabbet. The cutter will follow irregularities in the wood, so make sure the wood is perfectly straight.

MAKING A V-BLOCK

A V-block is useful for holding circular items steady while they are being worked on. Make the block from a length of 2 × 3in (50 × 75mm) S4S lumber – the actual length should be a little longer than the item to be held. The V is made to a depth of about 1in (25mm) in the 3in (75mm) side of the lumber. Cut the V using a circular saw with the blade tilted to 45°. Clamp the block firmly and fit the saw with a guide fence to keep the cut straight. Cut up one side and down the other. Practice on scrap wood while adjusting the depth and width of cut to give the correct size V-shape. Alternatively, you can use a V-cutter bit in a router. It may take two or three passes with the router to make the V to the full depth and width of the cutter.

PLANING

By hand Make sure that the plane blade is sharp and properly adjusted. Stand to one side of the work with your feet slightly apart so you are facing the work and feeling comfortable. Plane from one end of the piece of work to the other, starting the cut with firm pressure on the leading hand, transferring it to both hands, and finally to the rear hand as the cut is almost complete. Holding the plane at a slight angle to the direction of the grain can sometimes improve the cutting action.

With a power plane Remove ties and loose clothing; overalls are ideal. Wear goggles and a painter's mask. Turn the adjuster knob to set the depth to cut and start the plane. Begin with a shallow cut and increase the cutting depth if necessary. Make sure the work is clamped in place.

Stand comfortably to one side of the work and, holding the plane with two hands, set it into the work at one end and pass it over the surface to the other end. Push the plane forwards steadily; not too fast or you will get a wavy surface finish. When you have completed the work, switch off and make sure that the blades stop spinning before resting the plane down with the cutting depth set at zero.

DRILLING

To ensure that screwheads lie flush with the surface of plywood, particleboard or other material use a countersink drill bit.

To minimize the risk of splitting lumber, drill pilot and clearance holes for screws. For small screws, pilot holes can be made with an awl.

The **clearance hole** in the lumber should be fractionally smaller in diameter than the screw shank.

The **pilot hole** in the lumber to receive the screw should be about half the diameter of the clearance hole. The depth of the pilot hole should be slightly less than the length of the screw.

Drilling vertical holes To ensure vertical holes, mount the drill in a drill stand. If this is not possible, stand a try square on edge so that its stock (handle) is resting on the work alongside the drilling position, and the blade is pointing up in the air. Use this as a sighting guide and line up the drill as close as possible with the square to ensure the drill is vertical. It is also helpful if an assistant can stand back and sight along the drill and square from two sides to ensure the drill is held straight.

⑤ Making a V-block
Cut out a V in a block of 2 × 3in (50 × 75mm) lumber using a circular power saw tilted to cut at 45°.

⑥ Drilling Vertical Holes
With a drill stand, not only will the drill bit be held vertical, but depth is also controlled.

⑦ Freehand Drilling Guide
When drilling it can be helpful to stand a try square alongside the drill to ensure accuracy.

⑧ Drilling Depth Guide
There are various guides to control drilling depths, such as rings for drills, and masking tape.

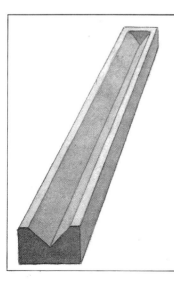

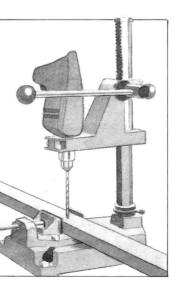

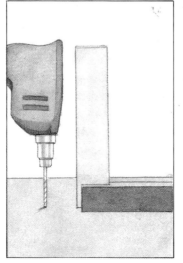

TECHNIQUES: WOOD JOINTS

WOOD JOINTS

Butt joint This is the simplest frame joint of all. The ends of the lumber to be jointed must be cut square so that they butt together neatly. Corner and "T" joints can be formed, which are glued and nailed for strength. Corrugated fasteners can also be used to hold these joints, especially where the sides of the frames will be covered to hide the fasteners. When "T" joints are being formed from inside a frame, they can be skew nailed (see page 84).

Corner joint This is a simple "knock down" fixture attached with screws; it is used to attach boards at right angles. They are described as "knock down" joints because some are in two parts for easy disassembly, and even the simple attachments can be unscrewed. They do not look very attractive, but are useful where they will be hidden – by a fascia, for example.

Miter joint Popular for making picture frames, but suitable for other

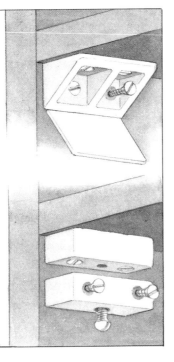

2 Corner Fitting Joints
Ideal for joining wood and boards at right angles. *Top* A one-piece fitting. *Bottom* A two-part type. Both are easily fitted using screws.

1 Simple Butt Joints
***Top* Corner and *below* "T" joints can be formed by skew nailing or by using corrugated fasteners.**

right-angled corner joints. Cut the joint at 45° using a miter box as a guide. A simple miter joint is glued and nailed, but a stronger joint can be made using dowels, or by making oblique saw cuts into which wood veneers are glued.

Half-lap joint Also known as halving joints, these join wood of similar thickness at corners or to form "T" or "X" joints (mid-lap and cross-lap joints). Cut each piece to half its thickness. Use a try square to mark the width of the cut-outs and a marking gauge set to half the thickness of the wood to mark their depth. Be sure to cross-hatch the waste wood with a pencil so that the correct side is removed. To form an end-lap joint, saw down as for making a tenon joint (see page 88). To form a mid- or cross-lap, saw down on each side of the "T" cut-out to the depth of the central gauge line, then chisel out the waste.

Dado joint Used mainly for shelving, this is basically a slot into which a shelf fits. The "through" dado joint

3 Types of Half-lap Joints
***Top* A corner-lap joint. *Bottom left* A mid-lap joint. *Bottom right* A cross-lap joint.**

4 Forming a Half-lap Joint in Lumber Battens
Mark width of the cut-out. Mark half the thickness of the wood with a marking gauge. Cross hatch area to be removed. Saw down sides with a back saw, then chisel out the waste.

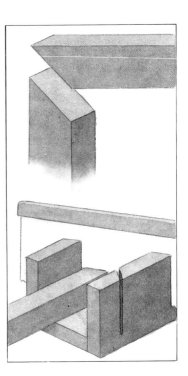

5 Cutting Miter Joints
Miters make right-angled corner joints. Using a miter box as a guide for ensuring a 45° angle, cut out the joint with a back saw.

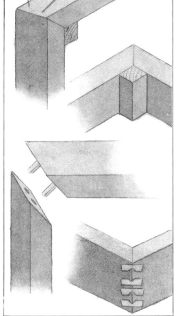

goes to the full width of the shelf, while a "stopped" dado joint is taken only part of the way across the board. Chisel the waste away from each side. In the case of a stopped dado, chisel the waste from the stopped end first. If you have a router, it is easier to cut a dado joint by running the router across the board against a batten clamped at right angles to the board to guide the router accurately.

A rabbet joint is similar to a dado joint at the top of a board, and can be cut in a similar way (*see* **Cutting rabbets, page 82**).

Bare-faced rabbet-and-dado joint This type of dado joint, used at the corners of a frame, is a much stronger joint than the common butt joint or lap joint because the rabbet of one piece is held in a dado cut in the other piece. The joint will be held just with good aliphatic resin wood-working glue, and by nailing or screwing down through the top into the upright. However, because of the short grain of the outside of the dado, this piece is left overlong while

the joint is made, and then the "horn" (the excess timber) is cut off neatly, flush with the side of the joint. The rabbet should be no thicker than half the width of the lumber being jointed.

Carefully mark out the joint with a utility knife, a try square, and a marking gauge. The depth of the dado (groove) should be about one-third to a half the thickness of the upright. Cut the sides of the dado to the required depth using a back saw held vertical, or a carefully set circular saw. Clamping a batten alongside the dado will help to keep the cut straight. Remove the waste with a chisel, working from both sides to the middle, and holding the chisel with the flat side downwards. Alternatively, cut the dado with a router (*see* **Cutting grooves and slots, page 82**).

Mark out the vertical piece so that the rabbet will exactly fit in the dado. Use a marking gauge to mark out the rabbet. The rabbet is cut with a router or with a hand saw and chisel to form the tongue (*see* **Cutting rabbets, page 82**).

---

6 Forming Miter Joints
Top Glue and nail together a simple miter joint. *Bottom* Reinforce the joint with a corner block, dowels, or wood veneer.

8 Types of Dado Joint
Top A through dado joint. *Middle* A through dado joint on the side of a central support. *Bottom* A corner dado joint.

7 Stages in Forming a Through Dado Joint
Mark width of the dado according to the thickness of the wood being joined. Use a utility knife. Mark depth with a marking gauge. Cut down the sides with a back saw. Chisel out the waste, working from both sides to the middle.

9 Stages in Making a Bare-faced Rabbet-and-dado Joint
Leave a "horn" of surplus lumber to support the short grain which will be on the outside of the groove. Mark width of piece being joined. Mark and cut dado as before. Saw off horn.

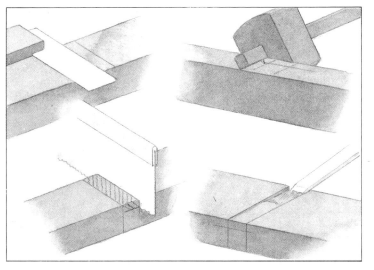

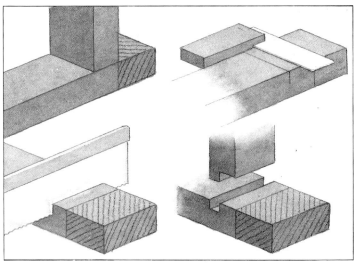

Techniques: Wood Joints

Mortise and tenon joint A mortise and tenon joint can be marked out with a mortise gauge. Mark out the tenon (the tongue) so that it is one-third of the thickness of the piece of wood. The mortise (the slot) is marked at the same width in the other piece. The length of the mortise should match the width of the tenon being fitted. Drill out most of the waste with a series of holes using a drill bit slightly smaller than the mortise width. Working from the center, chop out the mortise with a chisel to the depth required. If making a through joint (in which the end of the tenon is visible), turn the wood over and complete the mortise from the other side.

Hold the tenon piece upright, but sloping away from yourself, secure in a vise, and use a back saw carefully to cut down to the shoulder. Then swivel the wood around to point the other way, and saw down to the other side of the shoulder. Next, position the wood vertically and cut down to the shoulder. Finally, place the wood flat and saw across the shoulder to remove the

2 Marking and Cutting a Mortise and Tenon Joint
Mark the length of the mortise slot to match the size of the rail being joined. Set the mortise gauge to the width of the chisel being used to cut out the mortise slot. (Chisel should be about one-third the width of wood being joined.) Use the mortise gauge to mark the mortise, and also the tenon, on the rail. Drill out the mortise and complete the cut with a chisel. Use a back saw to cut out the tenon.

1 Mortise and Tenon Joints
Top A common or stopped mortise and tenon joint. *Below* Through mortise and tenon joint.

3 Making a Haunched Mortise and Tenon Joint
Leave rail over-long. Mark out as before but allow for shoulder at top. Cut mortise slot, then saw down sides of a shoulder. Finish mortise using a chisel. Cut tenon as shown.

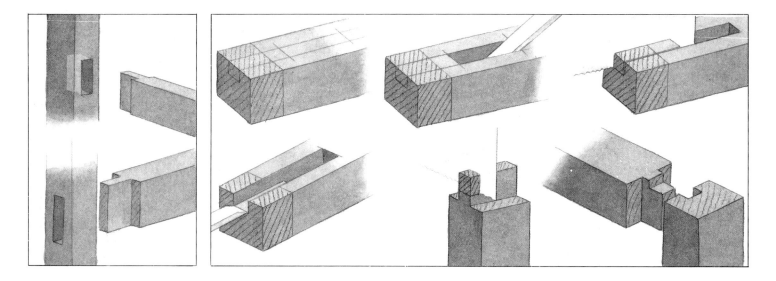

waste. Repeat for the waste on the other side of the tongue. Check that the two pieces fit well before gluing and assembling the joint. For added strength and a better appearance, cut small additional shoulders at each end of the tenon. If made accurately, these joints will withstand a lot of wear, and are capable of supporting a heavy load.

Haunched mortise and tenon joints   For joints at the corner of a large frame, or for joints that will have to support heavy weights, a square "haunch" or shoulder can be left in the tenon to increase its effective width and considerably strengthen the joint.

The joint is marked out with a try square, utility knife, and marking gauge as for an ordinary mortise and tenon, but allowance is made for a square shoulder at the top as shown in the diagram.

To prevent the small amount of cross-grain lumber above the mortise from being pushed out when the mortise slot is cut, the rail is left overlong at this stage to create a "horn"

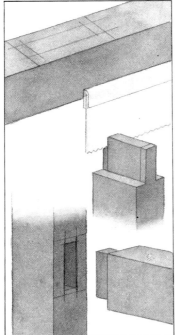

⑤ Shouldered Tenon Joint
For enhanced strength and appearance, cut small additional shoulders at each end tenon. Do this by sawing down.

④ Making a Bare-faced Mortise and Tenon Joint
Tenon is offset to one side. Mark and cut as shown here.

which is cut off after the joint has been made and assembled.

Bare-faced mortise and tenon joint   If the tongue of a tenon joint is offset to one side, this produces a bare-faced tenon as shown below (fig 4). This produces a strong joint which is very useful in cases where narrow rails meet the thicker rails of the main frame. The mortise slots in the frame rails can be cut farther back from the front edge for extra strength, and the bare-faced tenons of the narrow rails allow the front faces of these rails to lie flush with the front face of the main frame, giving a neat, secure finish.

A bare-faced tenon is cut in the same way as a half-lap joint (or halving joint).

Dovetail joint   A dovetail joint is made so that the "pins," which are the protruding fingers, interlock in both parts of the joint, giving a joint of great pull-out strength. The joint can only come apart in the same way as it was assembled.

A sliding bevel is used to mark out

a central dovetail pin on one rail, and the dovetail shape is cut out using a dovetail saw or fine-toothed back saw to leave a central pin.

The thickness and shape of the pin is marked on the other piece, called the "post," and the marks are extended on to the ends using a try square. The post is held upright and the waste inside the two outer pins is cut out using a dovetail saw, while a coping saw is used to cut across the bottom of the waste. The sides are pared down to size with a chisel.

⑥ Marking Out and Cutting a Dovetail Joint
Mark a line the thickness of the matching piece. Using a mortise gauge, mark top of the pin. Mark sides of pin with sliding bevel set at slope of 1 in 6. Cut pin with back saw. Hold pin on other piece. Mark dovetail and cut out waste with back and coping saws. Pare base accurately with chisel to achieve good fit.

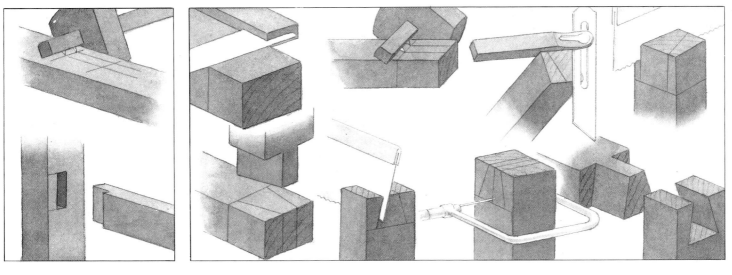

Dowel joint Dowels are a strong, simple, and hidden means of joining wood together.

Use pre-cut grooved dowels with beveled ends (*see* **Materials, page 78**). These range from ¼in (6mm) diameter by 1in (25mm) long to ⅜in (10mm) by 1½in (38mm). The dowel length should be about one-and-a-half times the thickness of the wood being jointed. If you need to use doweling of a larger diameter (as used in the cupboard door frames in the Tiled Kitchen or for the Alcove Shelves and Cupboards), cut your own lengths of dowel. Cut grooves down the length of dowel to allow glue and air to escape, and bevel the ends. The dowel lengths should be twice the thickness of the wood being joined.

On both pieces of wood, use a marking gauge to find the center line, and mark with a pencil. Drill the dowel holes to half the dowel length with the drill held in a drill stand, or aligned with a try square stood on end. Drill the dowel holes in one of the pieces to be jointed, insert center points in the holes, then bring the two pieces of the joint together so they are carefully aligned. The center points will make marks in the second piece of wood where the dowel holes should be drilled. Drill the holes to half the length of the dowels, plus a little extra for glue. Where dowels are used for location rather than strength, such as for joining worktops, set the dowels three-quarters into one edge and a quarter into the other.

Put glue in the holes and tap the dowels into the holes in the first piece with a mallet. Apply glue to both parts of the joint; bring them together and clamp them in position until the glue has set.

GLUING

All joints are stronger if glued. Make sure that surfaces to be joined are clean and well-fitting. Clamp surfaces together while the glue is setting, but not so tightly that all the glue is squeezed from the joint. Use waterproof glue for joints that may be subject to dampness. If the parts do not fit tightly, use a two-part resorcinol glue.

① Types of Dowel Joint
Dowels can join panels edge to edge and join frames at corners. They can be hidden or have ends exposed.

② Dowels to Join Panels
Right Mark dowel positions. Drill holes, insert center points. Mark second piece.

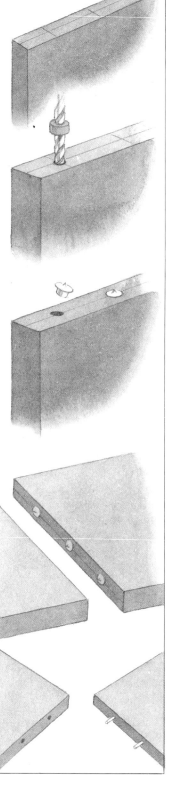

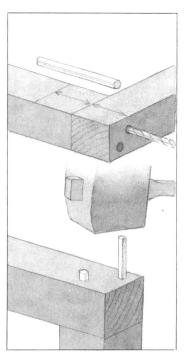

③ Making a Doweled Frame
If edge of frame will not be seen, drill holes for dowels after making frame. Hammer dowels home; cut ends flush after glue dries.

④ Using a Doweling Jig
If dowels are to be hidden, a doweling jig makes it easy to drill holes that align in both pieces.

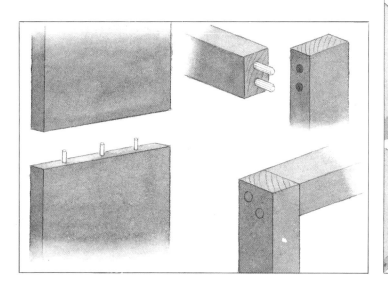

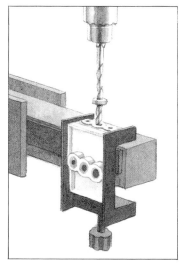

SCRIBING AND LEVELING

Scribing long lengths When you are fitting a worktop, horizontal panel, shelf, or vertical panel to a wall, you are likely to find that it will not touch the wall at every point since it is extremely unlikely that the wall will be flat and square. To avoid such gaps, it is necessary to scribe the item to the wall.

Hold the item in place and as close to its final position as possible. If it is a worktop, make sure that it is level and at right angles to whatever is next to it. If it is an upright, make sure that the front edge is held plumb. Where the gap is at its widest, pull the panel forward so that the gap is 1in (25mm). Take a block of wood 1in (25mm) long and place it on the panel, against the wall, at one end. Hold a pencil against the other end of the block, and draw the pencil and block along the wall so that the pencil makes a line, which reproduces the contours of the wall.

With a Saber saw or a compass saw, cut along the line. Where the line is too close to the edge to saw,

shape the panel to the line using a tool such as a Surform or a wood rasp. Press the panel against the wall and check that it fits neatly all the way along.

Scribing in alcoves It is more difficult to scribe in an alcove because a horizontal panel will usually fit neatly only *after* it has been scribed to the walls.

Using a large wooden square (you can make one from lumber battens following the 3-4-5 principle of producing a right-angled triangle [*see* page 80]), find out if one, or both, of the side walls are square and flat. If they are, you can carefully measure between them at the required height of the worktop. Then saw off the ends of the worktop to this length and position it, before finally scribing it to the rear wall as described above.

If the side walls of the alcove are not square, you can mark out the worktop using a cardboard template (*see* **Using templates**) of each side wall and part of the rear wall which you then scribe to fit.

Using a contour gauge This device (*see* **Tools, page 72**) is used for reproducing a complicated shape and is useful if you have to fit, for example, a worktop around something such as a decorative wood molding. It comprises a row of movable pins or narrow plastic strips held in place by a central bar. When pressed against a shape, the pins follow the outline of the shape. The contour gauge is then held on the item to be fitted and the shape transferred to it by drawing around the contour gauge with a pencil. After use, realign the pins.

Using templates When cutting around an awkward-shaped object, such as a pipe, it is a good idea to make a template of the obstruction. Make the template from cardboard or thick paper. Cut and fold the template to make it as accurate as you can. When you are satisfied that you have a good fit, place the template on the item to be fitted, and mark around it to produce a cutting line. Alternatively, glue the template in position and cut around it.

Leveling battens When attaching battens to a wall with masonry nails, first lay the battens on the floor and drive the nails almost all the way through them. On the wall, use a carpenter's level to position the batten horizontally and draw a pencil line along the top edge of the batten. Hold the batten in position and drive a masonry nail at one of the ends part of the way into the wall. Check that the top of the batten aligns with the guide line, then rest the carpenter's level on the batten and, with the bubble central, drive a nail into the wall at the other end of the batten. Make sure that the batten is level, then drive in all the nails.

If attaching the batten with screws, drill clearance holes in the batten as above and, with a pointed tool, mark the wall through a screw hole at one end of the batten. Drill and anchor the wall at this point (*see* **Wall fixtures, page 84**) then screw the batten to the wall. Level the batten as above, mark the other screw positions, then remove the batten and drill and anchor the wall. Finally, screw the batten in place.

⑤ **Scribing Long Lengths to Fit Against a Wall**
Where gap is widest pull panel forwards so gap is 1in (25mm). Hold pencil against 1in (25mm) wide block; move block and pencil along wall to draw cutting line. Cut along this line.

⑥ **Attaching Leveling Battens to a Wall**
If attaching with masonry nails drive these into battens first. Hold batten in place and mark wall. Holding batten on marked line, insert nail at end. Recheck level; drive in other nails.

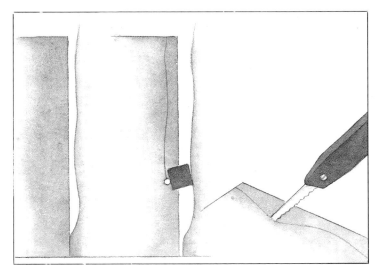

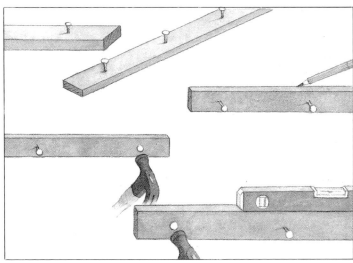

Leveling kitchen units Floors are rarely level, so that when installing kitchen units you must work from the highest spot in the room. Assemble the units and temporarily place them in position. Take a long, straight wooden batten and place this on the top of the units. Place a carpenter's level on the horizontal batten, to find the highest unit. Work from this unit and bring all the other units up to this level by shimming pieces of plywood or hardboard underneath them. After this is done, the worktops can be installed, and the inset sink connected.

Aternatively, if you have yet to construct the support units, you can build each one to the exact height required to compensate for differences in floor level. This leveling technique is very useful for old properties where floors are invariably uneven. First, lay straight battens around the floor where the units will be positioned – one batten at the front edge and one at the back. Work from the high point and shim the battens so that they are level. Mark on them the positions of the units and at each point measure the gap to the floor. Increase the height of each unit by this amount.

Finding verticals Use a plumb line to mark a vertical line on a wall. Tap a nail into the wall where you want the vertical to be, and tie the plumb line to it. When the line is steady, hold a scrap of wood on the wall so it just touches the string and mark the wall at this point. Repeat the procedure at a couple of other places. Alternatively, rub the plumb line with chalk. When it stops swinging, press it against the wall, then pluck the string to leave a vertical chalk line on the wall.

Hanging Doors

Hinged cupboard or wardrobe doors There are two ways to fit hinged doors; they can be **inset** to fit between side frames, or they can be **flush overlay** where the doors cover the side frames.

Inset doors look attractive, but they are harder to fit than flush overlay doors because they must be very accurately made to achieve a uniform gap all round the opening. Flush overlay doors cover the frame and hide any uneven gaps. Also, the concealed hinges that are normally used to hang a flush overlay door are adjustable, making it easy to alter the door so that it opens and closes correctly.

Fitting Hinges

Inset doors **Flush hinges** are the easiest to fit. They are simply screwed to the edge of the door and the frame, and require no recessing. However, they cannot be adjusted after fitting, so great accuracy is required. The inner flap of the hinge is screwed to the edge of the door, while the outer flap is screwed to the inner face of the frame.

Attach the hinges at equal distances from the top and bottom of the door. With a tall or very heavy door, fit a third hinge centrally between the other two. Mark the hinge positions on the edge of the door with the hinge knuckle (joint) in line with the door front. Drill pilot holes and screw on the inner flap. Hold the door in place or rest it on something to raise it to the correct height, making sure that it is accurately aligned at the top and bottom, and mark the positions of the hinges on the frame. Remove the door and extend these lines using a try square. Hold the door against the frame so it is in an open position, and screw the outer hinge flaps in place, so that they match up with the guide lines.

Butt hinges are conventional flapped hinges and are available in steel (commonly) or in brass, which is better for high quality work. They are attached in the same way as flush hinges, except that the hinge flaps have to be recessed into the lumber using a chisel or router.

Mark out the hinge positions as for flush hinges, making sure that the hinges are not positioned so that the fixing screws will go into the end grain of cross members and be likely to pull out.

The length of the hinges are marked out first, using a utility knife, then the width of the hinge and the thickness of the flap are marked using a marking gauge. With a chisel held vertical, and a mallet, cut

---

① Using a Contour Gauge
To reproduce complicated shapes, press the gauge against objects; use it as a pattern.

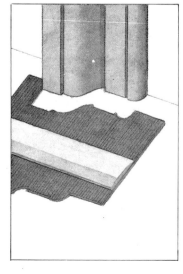

② A Method of Leveling Kitchen Units
Temporarily position the units or the partition frame. Place carpenter's level on a straight batten to find the highest unit. Pack plywood or hardwood pieces under other units to bring them to this height.

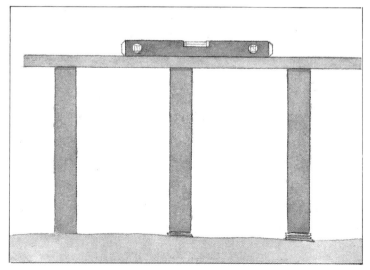

③ Fitting a Flush Hinge
Flush hinges are very easy to fit. Screw the outer flap to the frame and the inner flap to the door.

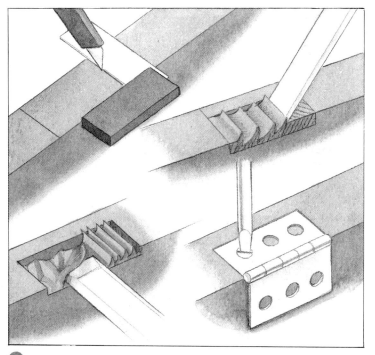

④ The Stages in Fitting a Butt Hinge

Using a try square and a utility knife, mark out the length of the hinge. With a marking gauge mark width and thickness of hinge flap. With chisel vertical, cut around outline of hinge. Make series of cuts across width of recess. Pare out the waste, then check that the flap lies flush. Once this is done, screw the butt hinge in place.

down around the waste side of the recess, then make a series of vertical cuts across the full width of the recess. Remove the waste by careful chiseling, then finally pare the bottom of the recess flat using the chisel held flat-side downwards.

If you are careful, you can remove the bulk of the waste from a hinge recess using a straight bit in a router. The bit is set to cut to the depth of the recess, and afterwards the corners can be finished off using a chisel.

Flush overlay doors Modern, adjustable **concealed hinges** are the most commonly used. There are many types available, and they come with full installation instructions. Some types are face-fitted and simply screw in place on the inside face of the door, but usually a special Forstner bit is used to drill a wide, flat-bottomed hole for the hinge body in the rear surface of the door. Next the base plate is screwed to the side frame. Finally, the hinge is attached to the base plate and the adjusting screws are turned until the door fits perfectly.

FITTING CATCHES

Many types of concealed hinges have built-in closers, so catches are not required. With conventional hinges, **magnetic catches** are popular. The magnet is fitted to the side of the cabinet and the catch plate is then positioned on the magnet. The door is closed onto the catch and pressed hard so that the catch plate marks the door. The door is opened and the catch plate is then simply screwed to the door.

Ball catches are very neat devices. On the central edge of the door a hole is drilled to accept the body of the ball catch, which is pressed into place. The door is closed and the ball marks the edge of the cupboard. The door is opened and the striker plate carefully positioned to coincide with the center of the ball. If you are recessing the striker plate, its outline should be drawn around, using a utility knife. The strike plate is then recessed into the cabinet so that it lies flush with the surface enabling the catch to operate smoothly.

⑤ Fitting Face-fixed Concealed Hinges

This hinge is simply screwed to the inside face of the door and frame.

⑥ Fitting Recessed Concealed Hinges

Blind hole is drilled for hinge body. The base plate arm is adjustable.

⑦ Magnetic Cupboard Catch

A magnetic catch is screwed to the inside face of a cabinet and the catch plate is screwed to the frame.

⑧ Fitting a Ball Catch

Drill door edge centrally for ball catch body which is pressed in place. Striker plate fixes to frame.

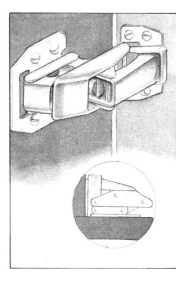

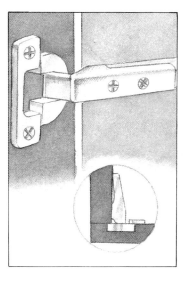

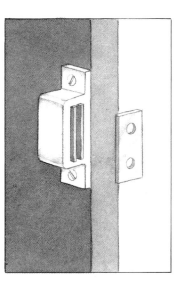

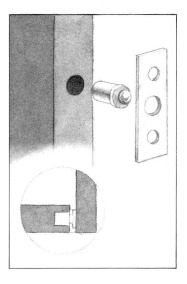

TECHNIQUES: TILING

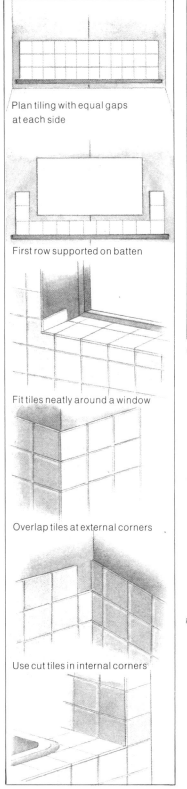

Plan tiling with equal gaps at each side

First row supported on batten

Fit tiles neatly around a window

Overlap tiles at external corners

Use cut tiles in internal corners

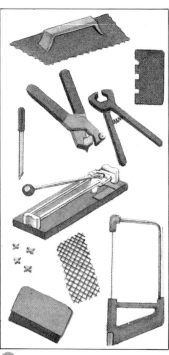

Planning When tiling, accurate laying out is essential. The tiles must be applied absolutely level, and, after tiling, no cut edges should show. Only factory-glazed edges, or half-round edge (bullnose) tiles which are made to be seen, should be visible. With the frames of the shower partition (page 22) note that the frame width is designed so that the front face tiles exactly cover the ends of the frames and the edges of the tiles glued to each side. Tiles on the side panels are arranged so that cut tiles are right at the back of the units. Similarly, if any tiles have to be reduced in height, these cut tiles should be at floor-level where they will be less noticeable.

When tiling a plain wall, centralize the tiles on it, using cut tiles of equal width at each end. If the wall has a prominent window, arrange the tiles to give it a neat border. In both cases, adjust the height of the tiles by having cut tiles at floor or baseboard level. Plan your tiling scheme so that part-tiled walls and low vertical surfaces, such as the side of a bathtub, have whole tiles on the

top row. You may have to compromise on the best overall arrangement for the room. To deal with window reveals (recesses), have glazed edges visible around the front of the reveal, and have cut tiles butting up to the window frame.

Laying out Start by making a gauging rod. This is simply a length of straight lumber about $\frac{1}{2} \times 1\frac{1}{2}$in ($12 \times 38$mm), on which pencil lines are drawn to indicate tile widths, including spacers. To mark the lines, lay out a row of tiles along the gauging rod, with spacers between them – unless tiles incorporating spacers are being used. Draw a line across the gauging rod to coincide with the center of each joint. If rectangular tiles are used, a second rod will be required for tile heights.

Use the gauging rod(s) to lay out accurately the tile positions. When you are satisfied with the arrangement, nail a straight lumber batten (about $\frac{1}{2} \times 1\frac{1}{2}$in [$12 \times 38$mm]) horizontally across the full width of the area to be tiled to support the first row of complete tiles. Next, nail vertical battens at each side to support

① Tools for Tiling
Top to bottom **Adhesive spreaders – metal and plastic; scoring tool; cutting pliers; tile nippers; heavy-duty cutter; spacers; file; saw; grout spreader.**

② Making a Gauging Rod
Lay out a correctly spaced row of tiles and on a batten accurately mark tile widths including spacers.

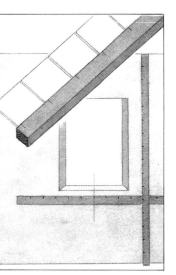

③ Setting out the Wall
Centralize tiles on a dominant feature like a window, and fix batten one tile height above floor.

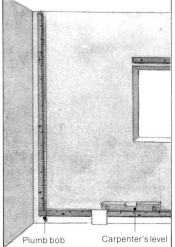

Plumb bob   Carpenter's level

④ Starting to Attach tiles
Also fix vertical battens at each side. Spread adhesive in corner and press tiles firmly into place.

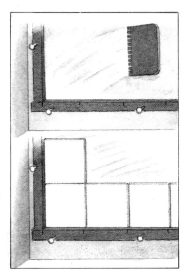

the last row of complete tiles at the sides and to keep the tiling square. Use the gauging rods to mark off on the wall battens the exact tile widths and heights, as this will help you to keep the tiling square. If you are tiling a plastered wall, nail the tiling battens with lightly driven-in masonry nails. If tiling on wood or plywood use common nails.

TILING TOOLS

Adhesive spreader A simple notched plastic tool which evenly spreads a bed of tile adhesive.

Tile cutter There are various types of tile cutters available. Some resemble a pencil and have a tungsten-carbide tip which is drawn across the tile to score the surface where the break is required. A better type is a cutter resembling a pair of pincers. This has a cutting wheel to score a cut line, as well as jaws between which the tile is placed before the cutter handles are squeezed, pincer-like, to make the cut. A heavy-duty cutter for thick, large tiles consists of a jig with a cutting-lever arm.

Tile saw Consists of a tungsten-carbide rod-saw blade fitted into a frame. It will cut tiles to any shape: L-shaped, curved, etc. The tile to be sawn is clamped in a vise.

Tile spacers Nowadays it is common for tiles to be supplied with plain edges, rather than with built-in spacer lugs molded on the edges of the tiles. Spacer tiles are simply butted together and are automatically evenly spaced as they are positioned. However, with plain edge tiles it is important to place spacers between the tiles as they are positioned. This creates even gaps for grouting between the tiles.

Tile nippers A plier-like device for removing narrow strips which are too small to be handled by a conventional cutter. It will also cut shaped tiles.

Tile-file Useful for cleaning up sharp and uneven edges of a cut tile.

Grout spreader Flexible rubber blade for spreading grout cement into joints.

Sponge For cleaning away adhesive and grout from the surface of a fixed tile.

Tiling process Establish tile positions by laying out, then begin tiling in a bottom corner and spread adhesive over about 1 square yard. Rake it out evenly using the notched spreader supplied with the adhesive. Working from a corner, press the tiles into the adhesive with a slight twisting motion. If tiles without spacers are used, hold them evenly apart with plastic wall-tile spacers. These can either be pressed well into the joints and left in place, or they can protrude from the surface, in which case they can be pulled out after an hour or so and re-used elsewhere. Fit whole tiles only: tiles cut to fit around obstacles can be fitted later.

Cutting edge tiles Wait for 12 hours after the main area of tiling has been completed, before removing the setting-out battens. Tiles can then be cut to fill the gaps around the perimeter. Measure the space into which the tile is to fit, remembering to allow for the spacers between tiles. Use a tile cutter to cut a straight line across the surface of the tile, then smooth rough edges using a tile file. Use a notched spreader to

apply adhesive direct to the back of the tile, and press it into place.

Cutting around difficult shapes To cut around a pipe, snap the tile along the center line of the pipe, then score the pipe's outline on the surface. For a neat finish, saw around the pipe outline using a tungsten-carbide rod-saw held in a conventional hacksaw frame. Alternatively, nip away the pipe cutout by snapping off small pieces of the tile, using tile nippers or a pair of pliers. Tiles to be laid around basins and window openings can also be scored along the cutting line and then nipped. Alternatively, the cutout can be sawn out, which is likely to avoid breakages if the part to be cut out is close to the edge of the tile.

Finishing off Once the tiles are firm they should be grouted with a waterproof grout applied with a rubber spreader. When the grout is just beginning to set, use a small rounded stick to press the grout into the joint lines, then wipe off the excess grout with a damp sponge. When the grouting has dried, polish the tiles' surface with a dry duster.

⑤ Cutting Tiles to Size
Score along glazed side, then break tile along line using a cutting tool. Saw awkward shapes.

⑥ Cutting Around Pipes
Mark position of hole on face of tile. Snap tile along center line. Score outline, then nip out waste.

⑦ Grouting Tiles to Finish
Use rubber blade squeegee to press grout into joints. As grout sets, press rounded stick along joints.

⑧ Drilling a Hole in Tiles
Stick masking tape on drill point. Use masonry drill bit. Switch to hammer action when tile drilled through.

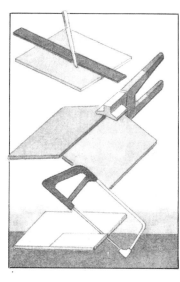
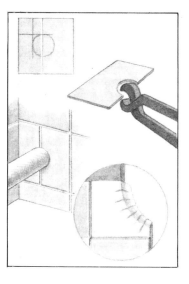
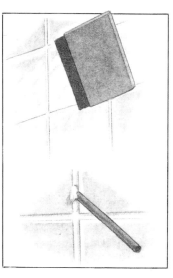
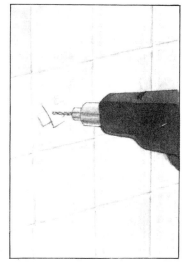

INDEX

ACKNOWLEDGMENTS

The publisher thanks the following photographers and organizations for their kind permission to reproduce the photographs in this book:

6 left Camera Press; **6** center Richard Bryant/Arcaid; **6** right Ken Kirkwood; **7** Simon Brown/Conran Octopus; **8** Karen Bussolini (House Beautiful Specials); **9** Aldo Ballo; **10** left Jean-Pierre Godeaut; **10** right Fritz von der Schulenburg; **11** left La Maison de Marie Claire (Sarramon/ Forgeur); **11** right Pascal Chevalier/Agence Top; **12** above Neil Lorimer/Elizabeth Whiting & Associates; **12** below left Rodney Hyett/Elizabeth Whiting & Associates; **12** below right Tim Street-Porter/Elizabeth Whiting & Associates; **13** above Tim Street-Porter/Elizabeth Whiting & Associates; **13** below left Elizabeth Whiting & Associates; **13** below center Lars Hallen; **13** below right Jean-Pierre Godeaut; **14–15** Jean-Paul Bonhommet; **16** above Richard Bryant/Arcaid; **16** below Tim Street-Porter/Elizabeth Whiting & Associates; **17** left Tim Street-Porter/Elizabeth Whiting & Associates; **17** right Jean-Pierre Godeaut (designer Lydia Kumel); **18** left Simon Brown/Conran Octopus; **18** right Rodney Hyett/Elizabeth Whiting & Associates; **19** Rodney Hyett/Elizabeth Whiting & Associates; **20** left & right Rodney Hyett/Elizabeth

Whiting & Associates; **21** Tim Street-Porter/Elizabeth Whiting & Associates; **22** above Rodney Hyett/ Elizabeth Whiting & Associates; **22** below left Andreas von Einsiedel/Elizabeth Whiting & Associates; **22** below right Simon Brown/Conran Octopus; **23** Tom Leighton/World of Interiors; **24** left Gary Chowanetz/Elizabeth Whiting & Associates; **24** right Jean-Paul Bonhommet; **25** left Vogue Living (Rodney Wiedland); **25** right Rodney Hyett/Elizabeth Whiting & Associates; **26** Rodney Hyett/Elizabeth Whiting & Associates; **27** Lars Hallen; **28** left Tim Street-Porter/Elizabeth Whiting & Associates; **28** right Christian Sarramon; **29** above Richard Bryant/Arcaid; **29** below left James Merrell/Homes and Gardens/Syndication International; **29** below center Elizabeth Whiting & Associates; **29** below right Belle (Geoff Lung); **68** Rodney Hyett/Elizabeth Whiting & Associates; **69** Camera Press; **70** Pascal Chevalier/Agence Top; **71** Belle (Neil Larimer).

Special Photography by Hugh Johnson and Simon Lee for Conran Octopus.

Hugh Johnson 30–37, 59, 60–61

Simon Lee 46–57, 66–67